Fearless Real Estate Book 2

THE Productive AGENT

Maximize Your Time and Profit by Mastering Cutting-Edge Virtual Tools

IVANIA ALVARADO

Become a Successful Residential Real Estate Agent and Maximize Cutting-Edge Virtual Tools to Impress and Educate Your Clients

Get more Buyers, Tenants, Sellers, and Landlords by leveraging online tools like Zoom and Google Meet from the first contact to the final transaction.

Thanks

God, Who has given me the opportunity to express myself.

My parents, Joseph and Mary, who taught me love and unconditional kindness.

My children, Sophia, Stephanie, and Alexander, my true inspirations in life, who motivate me each day.

My brothers, Raquel and Armando, whose unconditional support showed me the way to the truth.

A special thanks go to everyone I interviewed. Thank you for your collaboration and trust and for sharing your advice for success in the real estate business.

Contents

Introduction

The Productive Agent (Book 2 in the Fearless Real Estate series) shares the steps you can take as a new (or recommitted) real estate agent, so you can experience resounding success in your national and international profession. It's an excellent guide for new agents who are just starting out, as well as agents with experience who want a 180-degree change in their life and business. New agents will gain vast experience and knowledge, while brokers can use this guide to assist their agents in breaking through current income ceilings. I recommend first reading book 1 (*The Fearless Agent*) to understand and get a good start in the real estate business. Then agents will be ready to put into practice everything they learn in book 2 and be more prepared to receive new and more valuable information.

The qualities I suggest agents adopt and the teachings I describe will show readers a proven path to success. In this book, I recommend theories and practices brokers can encourage their agents to apply, and brokers can use this manual in their company as a study guide.

The Productive Agent is dedicated to the real estate agent who wants to be active in their business and live a better life. This book will cover how to sell through Zoom, Google Meet, or any other virtual platform, starting from the first interview all the way through closing the deal. I include a sample PowerPoint listing and marketing presentation.

Book 2 is a training manual so agents can immediately start working with buyers, tenants, landlords, and sellers. It is a crash course and a boot camp for your success all in one. Be ready to learn how to achieve your desired success.

What you will learn:

- The basic principles for several contract types
- Telemarketing
- How to work with Zoom and Google Meet
- How to use social media to advertise
- How to delegate
- How to prequalify all your clients so you don't waste time working with ghost clients
- Online marketing
- How to sell faster and be a great closer
- Bonuses include an open house form, buyer, seller, landlord, and tenant checklists, and much more!

Chapter 1

Working with Buyers

Buyers Who Are Ready, Willing, and Able

Before you start working with a buyer, you should learn to read their signals. Have a couple questions you can ask that will quickly tell you if working with this person will be worth your time. Many people will not become buyers for you or any other agent because they do not know what they want. Usually, agents with little experience or with few customers will waste their time on these types of clients.

Remember: Your time is valuable, and you should only work with buyers who will produce the results you want in a reasonable timeframe.

A ready, willing, and able person is the one who wants to buy today, not tomorrow. If the client wants to buy in a year, it is not wise to dedicate all your time now to helping them make a purchase. Since they're a potential future customer, maintain contact with them, but don't make them your priority today. Instead, learn to classify urgency on the part of the buyer in your favor.

A ready buyer is ready to buy now and will not waste their own time or yours. You will know their readiness by the way they answer and react to your questions. For them, buying is urgent.

A willing buyer will make immediate decisions and will not lose out on opportunities that are presented to them. They will make an offer immediately on a property that fits their needs. They are willing to buy in the present, not in the future.

An able customer is prepared with pre-qualification, pre-approval, or, better yet, wants to buy with cash. They may also be using a 1031 exchange and have sold a property and must locate a new property within 45 days that is equal to or greater than the price of the original property.

Never work with a buyer who is not yet prequalified, as it can be a waste of your time. Remember, time is money. If you waste your time, it can change the success of your business, your ability to reach your goals, and your overall passion for your business.

Here are some basic questions you should ask your prospective client to know if they are ready, willing, and able. You can ask them over the phone first, then if they are serious, you can meet them in person or on a virtual appointment. I recommend a virtual appointment if they are ready, willing, and able, because you can view properties together in Zoom at the same time, and your client will better understand how the market is reacting.

1. Are you prequalified or qualified for your purchase or investment? Yes_____ NO_____

   If the answer is Yes: Please email your prequalification letter to me or send your proof of funds (if the client is buying with cash).

   If the answer is No: Why not? OR, When do you plan on becoming prequalified?

   Then you can tell them to apply at their bank or refer financing companies.

2. When do you plan on moving or making your purchase? _____

3. How important is it for you to buy and/or move quickly on a 1-10 scale, with 1 being the least important and 10 being the most? _____

4. Are you the only person who decides about the purchase of this property? Yes_____ NO_____

   If the answer is No, ask: Who else is involved in this decision? _____

   What is their relationship to you? _____

The more you know, the better you will understand their needs and whether they're prequalified. This will save you time.

Tell them that everyone who makes a buying decision will need to be present when you show them a property.

5. If I find you the house of your dreams, would you make an offer immediately? Yes____ NO____

    If the answer is no: What would stop you from making an offer immediately?

_____

6. What percentage down payment do you have, or will you buy your home in cash?

_____

Prequalification

Prequalifying a customer is the number one step an agent must do. It is the best way to know what they can and want to purchase. You should know the basics for how to prequalify a buyer, even if you are not a loan originator. You'll want to know if a person qualifies and for how much.

Have several lenders, banks, and mortgage companies that you trust to refer to your client. Talk to them and work out a mutual referral system so you can refer business to them, and they can refer business to you.

Looking for the Right Property for Your Clients' Needs

Learning how to look for the perfect property for your client involves the art of listening. In the first interview with your new client, establish their prequalified status, explain what they will need to email you, and how you will work together before you start looking for properties. Your first interview can be in person, on the phone, or through Zoom.

You can work with your client on Zoom and use the sharing option on the MLS to find the right properties and areas they want. When you save the selections, your clients will receive an email of every new property with the options they picked.

Some agents go straight into showing the properties. That is a mistake, since they haven't created parameters with their clients and don't know how they want to be treated. You want to know exactly what your clients want and educate them on how the market is performing. If you do not qualify them, you stand to lose time, money, your motivation, and gas!

Here are the reasons you should conduct a first interview. The first interview could be in Zoom, Google Meet, over the phone, or in person:

1. It helps to break the ice by creating trust and rapport between you and your customers. This will help you create loyal customers who will not leave you to work with another agent. The time you invest with them will be remunerated at the end with a closing transaction and referrals.
2. They can give you any information and documentation they have, such as their prequalification letter, when you meet them in person or via Zoom or Google Meet. They could also email their documents to you before the meeting if it is over the phone.
3. Tell them about current market prices and how the market is performing. For example, is it a sellers' or buyers' market?
4. Explain how you work. Tell them if you are interested in only working exclusively or if you're open to a nonexclusive agreement.
5. Search for the properties together, so they understand the current property values in the market.
6. Use the "dream home" method. Explain to the buyer that they can place anything they want in a house without constraint. They can have up to ten characteristics, ordered from most important to least. For example:
   a. 4 bedrooms
   b. 3 bathrooms
   c. Double car garage
   d. Porte-cochère
   e. Pool
   f. Yard size
   g. Type of kitchen and design
   h. Family room
   i. Laundry room
   j. Courtyard roof
7. Write down everything the clients bring up while you are in the search. See if you can select any of these features since you know they will interest them.

8. Then, ask them: What are the top three or four features that you need at minimum to buy a house? If the house does not have these three or four features, you could neither buy it nor live in it. (Then keep quiet and listen to what they say.)

You can ask them to fill out this form in your first interview then have it ready when you show them properties. You could ask them to give it to you when you show them properties for the first time, since it will help them to decide and make the offer easier and faster. You can also send the form by email so the clients can fill it out in advance.

Showing Homes Ready to Make Contract

This form will help guide you and allow you to get references from your customers. Clients can give you references with the form or without if you explained the steps above to them.

Form to Choose the Property and Get References

Form for Buyers/Tenants
Name: _____ Date: _____
Address: _____
Email:
Telephone:
Property that interested you: _____
1st property
How did you like this property? _____
2nd property
Between this property and the previous one which do you like the most?
_____
3rd and last property
Between this and the one you have liked which one do you prefer?
_____
Perfect, I see that the one you liked the most was: _____
Would you like for me to go over the numbers of this property with you?
_____
Do you prefer to go to my office, or should we do it right here?
_____
Excellent. On a scale of 1-5, what is your level of interest in this property? 1 2 3 4 5
What would change your level of interest to a 5? _____
References

Name	email	Phone

This form will help you close the deal and write a contract faster through the process of elimination and the asking questions method.

1. Ask questions, starting from the first property. How did this property seem to you? (Keep quiet and listen.)

_____

_____

2. In the second property, ask: Between this house and the previous one, which house you think is better?

_____

_____

- Keep asking questions until you get to the last property.
- After you show the last property and the clients know which properties they like, you can ask them to go somewhere to prepare the contract or review the conditions of the property to see if they are qualified to purchase it and what is a good offer. For example: Can we go to your house, my office, or stay right here and see if you are qualified for this property and see what kind of offer you feel comfortable doing?
- Place the real estate contract alongside the property listing and a blank sheet of paper to record information about the property such as the down payment, a possible offer, a comparable in the area, and more. Then complete the contract immediately as you see and hear the clients give you green light signals. Keep writing until they sign and initial each page. Remember to use the option method rather than yes or no questions. For example: Do you prefer to give a $5,000 initial deposit or $10,000? If the buyer chooses one of your options, it means they're sending you a green light signal to write the contract.
- The process of writing the contract can be in any way you feel the most comfortable, either digital or on paper. The most important thing is to just do it.

Exclusive or Non-Exclusive?

Each agent must make the decision of whether to work with their buyers exclusively or non-exclusively. This is especially important when your client is truly ready, willing, and able to make a purchase.

You should always have an exclusivity agreement on hand since some buyers will be willing to work with you exclusively. Download the agreement from the program Form Simplicity under Exclusive Buyer Brokerage Agreement or use the tools that your broker provides.

Client Generator System

When creating marketing for your business or a property with the aim of attracting buyers, sellers, or whatever you want, you need to know what your goals are. Before putting a notice in the mail or sending it via social media, keep the following questions in mind:

- Who will read this notice? (Know who you will attract.)
- Who will respond to this type of notice?
- Why do I post ads like this?
- What do you want these ads to do for you, whether in social media, newspapers, magazines, etc.?

There are several ways to create your own system for marketing. While the following are some of the most common, being creative is great for your business:

1. Create a habit of calling prospective clients.
2. Hand out your business cards.
3. Ask for references.
4. Advertise with pamphlets.
5. Advertising in various places such as newspapers, websites, blogs, YouTube, magazines, and more.
6. Go to networking events.
7. Do informative free conferences.
8. Join clubs that will help your career.
9. Create a prospect list.
10. Be creative and build your own system.

Script: Finding Buyers in a List of Tenants in an Area

You: Hello _____, my name is _____ and I work with _____. I am a real estate agent. The reason for my call is to find out how many people are renting in our area, and I would like to be of help with the purchase of your home. Do you own a home or rent?

Them: _____

You: Perfect. Are you interested in knowing what new programs are available today for first time buyers or people who want to buy?

Them: Yes _____ No _____

*If he/she said **yes**:

You: Excellent. What day would be more convenient for us to talk about buying your home: Tuesday or Friday? And who would need to be there for an appointment in my office or via Zoom or Google Meet?

Them: _____

You: Good! Talk with you then.

*If he/she said **no**:

You: Do you know of anyone who is interesting in buying, selling, or renting that you can give them my phone, or you can give me their phone?

Them: _____

*Before meeting the clients, be sure to prequalify them on the phone to know if it is worth meeting them and showing them any properties. You must tell them they first need to prequalify through a bank or lender. If they do not know a mortgage company, you can provide a list of two or three mortgage companies that have a reciprocal referral agreement with you to increase your clientele.

Script: Calling Buyers from Referral

You: Hello, _____, my name is _____. You do not know me, but your name was given to me by a friend in common _____. He/she told me to call you.

_____ told me that I could help you with the purchase of your home since you are thinking of buying a property. He/she told me to call you, as he/she wants you to be in good hands and for that reason I am calling you.

How long have you been thinking about buying? _____

Are you working with any agents? Yes _____ No _____

Them: No.

You: Perfect! Are you prequalified? Yes _____ No _____

Have you gone to any financial institutions? _____

The best thing for us to do is to make an appointment through Zoom or Google Meet or for you to come to my office so I can better explain all the procedures involved in buying, as well as the requirements needed. Do you think Tuesday or Thursday would be better for you?

Them: _____

Excellent! I'll see you _____ at _____.

Telemarketing

This job is one of the most effective, if not *the* most effective and its cost is only your time. You can also hire someone to do it for you. The person must mention they are your assistant who works for you and the real estate company.

You can partner with another agent who makes the calls and qualifies the clients and then you show and close the deals. It is better to divide the work if you do not like one or the other side of the process. Some agents do not like to call but are good closers and others are good at getting clients, but do not like to show properties. If you do not like to do the calls or do not have the time or have grown so much, that is the time for an assistant or a partner so you can be more successful.

Cold Calls

Cold calls are calls to strangers. Several companies sell lists of prospects such as Bresser, Redx, Realtor.com, Zillow, and more. These people do not know you and you don't know them, and that is why they're called cold calls.

Warm Calls

Warm calls are to the references of your friends, customers, family, or you have approached them by giving them your business card or advertisement. There is a connection either by yourself or by someone else. They will feel they know you, so it makes the approach warmer, and they will usually feel a little more comfortable. For that reason, it is important to ask for references with all your customers, friends, and family to expand your database and to have faster results through warm calls.

Hot Calls

Hot calls are through your closest circle, your neighbors, family, friends, co-workers, the doctor, attorney, accountant, etc. You already maintain a direct relationship with them. Even if they are not interested in buying, selling, or renting, you should call them for their references. They are your first database and the people you will invite for your first business opening event.

Social Media (Facebook, Instagram, Twitter, Pinterest, LinkedIn and More)

Some agents have two accounts on their social media, one for friends and family and another for their business. Even if you have both accounts, be sure to keep healthy posts on each that will not hurt your reputation. Many of your customers will check your social media/networks to find out who you are.

75% of your posts should be related to growing your database, keeping your friends informed of the latest in real estate, and focused on increasing your followers. Post every new listing and open house as well as any price changes, new programs, and useful information about the market.

Some brokers hire a person or a social media marketing company to promote their business through social media. Learn how to do it yourself, hire someone else to do it, or have your real estate partner handle social media. The most important thing is to just do it.

Television

TV is more expensive than other forms of marketing, but it has many benefits if you can afford it. It will result in many customers. You can divide your commercial types into different demographic groups, do short commercials, or create a paid program for TV. You could find sponsors who can reduce your costs or share the program with sponsors when you buy a paid time slot.

Radio

The cost for radio is much lower than television and is also effective, whether it's a prepaid program or a short commercial, on AM or FM. You can do the spot alone, in a group, or with your company. Ask your broker if they want to participate or find sponsors to support your program. The cost could potentially be small, zero, or you could even make a profit, depending on how much you charge your sponsors.

Ads

Ads can be great sources of leads for agents who prefer to be called instead of initiating calls. Ads can make you known in the marketplace. While all kinds of ads can be useful, before you spend money, research the company's results and distribution compared to what you will pay. You'll want to know the publication's circulation numbers, where it is distributed, and how it can improve and expose your business to new clients. Try not to make long-term contracts when you first start advertising, so you can prove which outlet is better and not be tied to one without results.

Example of an effective direct advertisement to attract the desired prospect:

Coconut Grove-Beautiful, quiet, tree-lined neighborhood. All kinds of properties, prices (add a beautiful photo and an address of a house you're listing or ask permission to advertise another agent's listing).

Call now! Free list of homes 305-555-4444.

Your Name, Your Realty, Inc.

www.grovehouse.com

This type of advertisement will attract more prospects in the area you want to market, both buyers and sellers, at the desired price point. If for some reason the property is not what they are looking for, they can still call you to ask about the free list you're offering in the ad. They will already know they need to give you their information so you can send the list, then put them in your database and email distribution.

When you write your ad, use phrases like free, complimentary, no obligation, without pressure, and risk-free, to lower the pressure on your prospects so they have confidence when they call.

Real Estate Magazines

These magazines are good for listing agents to show the properties they have for sale, to sell themselves, or to have greater exposure to get more listings. Brokers use them to advertise among the other agents in the area or to recruit more agents. Buyers' agents use them to entice buyers to call about a specific program. They choose a property from their office and ask the listing agent for permission to advertise their listing.

Some of real estate magazines are:

- *Real Estate Magazine*
- *National Real Estate Investors*
- *Realty Times - Real Estate News and Advice*

- *Realtor*
- *Ocean Home*
- *Luxury Real Estate Magazine*
- *Unique Homes*
- *Urban Land*
- *Development Magazine*
- And more!

Example to Attract More Customers in a Specific Area

> **For information on any property in Coconut Grove:**
>
> **WWW.FINDMYHOUSE.COM**
>
> **Your Name; Your Realty**

> **Looking for a home?**
>
> **Go to: www.findmyhouse.com**
>
> **Your Name; Your Realty
> 305-444-4444**

> **Free!**
>
> **Certificate of valuation for your property
> www.Myhousevalue.us**
>
> **Your Name; Your Realty**

YouTube

YouTube is extremely important for every agent, plus it's free! You can upload a video of each listing you have to explain everything about the property. People can easily search for you or any of your ads or properties, and search results will show up in Google and other search engines. You embed your YouTube video on your website, text a link to your customers, post it on social media, and more.

Open a YouTube channel either just for yourself or with your team or your broker. This channel will help you get more of your desired clients. Before you open your YouTube channel, ask these questions:

1. What types of clients do you want to attract?

_____

_____

   When you know your target clients, you will be able to customize the subjects you will discuss on your channel.

2. What do you want to accomplish by starting your YouTube channel?

   Money _____, Listings _____, Buyers _____, Tenants _____

3. Do you want to do this yourself or have others help you? Who would you want to partner with? Another agent or your broker? _____

4. What advantages and disadvantages do you see in having a YouTube channel?

_____

_____

5. What subjects will you discuss in your YouTube channel? Create a list of subjects:

_____

_____

_____

6. Will your channel be an informative news channel, or will you just show your listings and open houses?

_____

7. What name will you choose for your YouTube channel? Create a list of names:

_____

_____

8. How often will you record and go live?

_____

_____

9. How much time can you dedicate to your YouTube Channel?

_____

_____

How to Upload a Video to YouTube:

For the most up to date information, go to YouTube to find a help button and/or search the videos they have on how to do your channel, create videos, and more:

1. Go to YouTube and search: how to upload videos on YouTube, from phone, on Tik-Tok, on YouTube from iPhone, on Instagram, on Pinterest, on Google drive, on WhatsApp, and more. Select the video you want.
2. Choose the most recent explanatory video that explains current changes in the system.

Edit Videos

On YouTube, search for "How to edit YouTube videos."

Here are some free video editors you can use for all your videos, not just for YouTube but also for your website, social media, and more:

1. Ice-cream Video: Good for editing.
2. MiniTool Movie Maker: Several templates, transitions, filters, etc.
3. Shortcut: Good for a better-quality image and audio that diminishes noise, more complex.
4. Open Shot: Easier than the others, has a blender.
5. Video Grabber: Good animation, background music, transitions, contains a big library.

Website

Most boards of realtors provide websites to their members as part of their membership fee, and you likely are represented on your real estate company's website. However, it is good to have a website of your own for various reasons. Since *you* are your business, your website serves as branding for you specifically that you can keep if in the future you decide to create your own real estate company. You maintain control of your client lists and how you manage your page and what you want to put there.

Texts

Text message marketing has become more advanced recently. You can work with companies that send mass texts by area, income, and other criteria. You can use a service like this or send your texts manually.

The message must be brief and direct for it to be effective. Use some of the examples in this manual or design messages that are specific to your desired prospects.

Chapter 2

Working with Sellers

When you list properties, you have the potential to earn double commissions when you sell or rent the property yourself, making listings an ideal situation. You control the transaction, and you can get many buyers from for sale signs and through the internet. When you list a property in the MLS, you will be exposed to hundreds of websites that generate buyers and tenants.

If you want to specialize as a listing agent, you need to create a referral system or partner with another agent who works with buyers and tenants, so you don't lose any prospects. If you plan on working with both buyers and sellers, you won't need to do this.

If you do want to specialize, you must be tenacious and invest in a farming system to gain leads in specific subdivisions as well as technology. Buy prospect lists of expired listings, for sale by owner (FSBO) properties, landlords, and foreclosures.

Plan on making calls consistently at least three or four days a week, if not every day.

After selling a house, always ask the seller where they are moving. Get their new contact details and continue to send them information at least every four to six months. Past customers are the best at referring another customer, plus they might be interested in buying again. Categorize them in your database so you can easily identify them as past customers.

You will work fewer hours with a seller than with a buyer. If you dedicate yourself to being a selling agent, you have more properties and transactions sold. According to studies, you will spend a quarter of the time working with sellers as you do with buyers.

How to Get More Listings

Create a system of calls, notices, social media, ads, email, farming, referrals, addressing/approaching people, blogs, YouTube, and more. Above all, be persistent in everything you do, but especially in the programs you choose. Diversify your activities and be tenacious. Buy lists in various places.

When you start, start with one program or system at a time and perfect it. If it works for you, do not change it unless it stops working.

Listing Presentation

There are several factors you will need to consider before a presentation:

*Some agents like to have a pre-listing package presentation and send it to the owner by email or leave it at the door of their house. This is a generic brochure for every seller who gives you an appointment so they will have an idea of how you work, who you and your company are, and your level of professionalism. You can also provide answers to common questions they may have before the listing presentation.

How to start your listing presentation:

*Start by breaking the ice and create rapport, then ask them to show you the house. Compliment the property when you see areas you really like or that will appeal to a buyer. It might be the patio, the neighborhood, or the kitchen. Make sure whatever you say is genuine; if you lie, you may sound insincere.

If they are nice and open to you, ask if you can start taking pictures of their property. When they say yes, this is a green light for you. Taking pictures will help you find more things to talk about their property before talking about the listing agreement and your commission.

On the day of the presentation, you must bring the listing presentation where you talk about:

1. You (resume) and your company
2. Marketing plan (where and how you will market their property, your plan). Example: Number and names of websites (Zillow, realtor.com..., MLS, social media, and more). Miami Board of Realtors has a list of around seven hundred websites to promote all listings, so

print the list and take it with you to show them. If you do not know how to get the list, call your board, and ask them how to find it on their website.

3. Questionnaire for sellers of how they want to sell their property. Example:

   Do you want me to do an Open House?

   Yes _____ No _____

   Do you want me to advertise your property on all the websites, social media, and ads?

   Yes _____ No _____

   How do you want to communicate? Text, phone, email, Zoom, WhatsApp, Google Meet.

   What are the best days and times to show the property? _____

   Phone and name of the person in charge of doing or accepting the appointment?

   _____   _____

   Is the property vacant or occupied? _____

   Do you want to use a lockbox combination, electronic, or key? _____

   If the property is rented, when does the lease expire? Or is it a month-to-month lease?

   Add more questions to find out about the association dues, pet restrictions, and so on.

4. Bring the correct listing agreement for the type of transaction you will do: a listing agreement for sale, for lease, for commercial properties, for vacant land, or for a business opportunity.

5. Reports from at least 2 different types of comparable programs (example: RPR, IMAPP, CMA) to give to them an estimate of the sales price. Remember, they always decide what the sales price will be. Put the recommended sales price on the last page because it is the last thing you will show before starting the agreement.

6. Tax roll/IMAPP to verify they are the owners.

7. Create a CMA List of properties for sale: active with contract, sold, pending, and expired in your area to show the sales prices for their neighbors. Use a marker to highlight the days they have been on the market so you can easily see which ones are overpriced. Do the same with the rest of the list. This will make them aware of the importance of putting the right price on a property. See next steps for more specific ways of explaining the correct pricing strategy.

8. List of expired properties to show them the days the other listing was for sale and was not sold to create a price relationship in line with reality.

9. Listing of properties pending contract. This shows that buyers usually bid below the price the owner wants. These prices are generally less compared to expired listings.

10. List of properties that were sold within the last six months. The owner will see how it was sold, the days the property was on the market, and the offer the buyer made to the seller. This will help your client be open for offers.

11. After you have shared comparable prices, take out the estimated price and tell them they decide how to price their house. Ask them: At what price are you planning to sell? *(Do not talk!)* $ _____

12. If for some reason the seller does not want to give you their property to sell, offer the **easy exit program.**

Example of a page that should be in all your listing presentations:

‹EXIT›

EASY EXIT!

Sale Agreement

What are you most worried about? Being tied to an agreement when your agent is not doing their job, and you can't get out of the contract.

I have the solution. When you work with (Your Name) with the EASY EXIT PROGRAM, you can cancel at any time without waiting for the end of the contract at no cost.

- You can cancel your agreement at any time.
- You are not tied to a contract. You can cancel if you decide you are not happy.
- Have confidence as I give you that peace of mind.

I believe if my client is not happy and/or satisfied with my work, you can THROW ME OUT.

_____   _____

Sign your name   Date

Telemarketing/Calling

See chapter 1 pages 20 and 21 for more information

Script: Calling Sellers for Sale by Owner (FSBO)

You: Hi, I am calling about your house for sale. Are you still selling it?

Them: Yes _____ No _____

You: My name is _____ with (company name) _____ .
Is your name (use the name that listed as the owner on the FSBO sign or look it up on the public record) _____ ?

The reason I am calling you is because I work with many buyers and sellers in your area, and I want to see how I can help in the sale of your property.

Usually, they will tell you **to bring the buyer.** If they do that, you should **answer:**

You: If I bring you a qualified buyer would you cooperate with a realtor?

Them: Yes _____ No _____

You: Perfect (always respond with something affirmative and positive). How long will you try to sell your home on your own until you decide to examine other options?

Them: _____

You: I get it. After you sell your house, where do you plan to move?

Them: _____

You: Good. How soon do you want to move?

Them: _____

If they have longer, you can tell them that now is the perfect time to sell their home at the best price. If it is a short time to move (if they must move out fast):

You: Why have you made the decision to move?

Them: _____

You: I see. (Seller's name), on a scale of 1-5 how would you measure your interest in selling your home?

Them: _____

You: Excellent! What kind of marketing strategy will you be using to attract buyers?

Them: _____

If they are not doing any advertising or investment, you can help them. Talk about the websites you have access to as a real estate agent. (Remember to print the list of websites that your board uses to promote your listings in addition to the MLS to show that you will invest on all these websites because you are paying the board and it is part of your membership fee.) You also have access to magazines, social media campaigns, and more. Tell the seller everything you use without focusing on any one thing, leaving them interested in more information.

If they say they have invested in marketing, respond by telling them they don't spend money with you unless you sell the house. If a seller invests in each of the platforms you use to promote your listings, it will cost them a fortune. If they work with you, they won't pay anything in marketing until you sell their property.

You: Why did you decide to sell your home on your own instead of hiring the services of a real estate professional?

Them: _____

If they say it's to save the commission fee:

You: I understand. I thought the same way as you before I became a real estate professional, but now I realize that it is the opposite. A seller earns more if they have an agent represent them. An agent not only represents you, but also sells the property at the best and highest possible price with the best qualified client, so you don't waste time and money.

You: If I show you with numbers that you will be better off with me selling your house, would this be something that would catch your attention?

Them: _____

You: How did you determine the sale price of your property?

Them: _____

You: Well, I would love to bring you an analysis of properties comparable to your property that's more up-to-date and with several programs that I have specialized in for your subdivision. Is the price you set firm or flexible?

Them: _____

You: Excellent. (Seller name), If I can help you sell your house at the highest possible price in the desired time, is this something you would be interested in?

Them: _____

You: If I can help make this happen, this would be okay with you, right?

Them: _____

You: Excellent. When would be a better time for us to speak in person? Could it be Monday or Wednesday?

Them: _____

You: Very well, I will see you on Wednesday. Do you think it is better in the morning or the afternoon?

Them: _____

You: Excellent, I will see you on (day) _____ at _____.

This is an example. Depending on how the seller responds, you will respond as well. The important thing is to have a clear idea of the possibilities.

Remember that you are deaf to **NO**, and you only accept **yes**. Make it easy for your prospect to answer yes to your questions (by avoiding answers that result in them saying no). Approach the conversation by putting yourself in their shoes, and always be on their side. When you share examples about other successful clients, you should always be the agent in the example or use the story of another agent's client.

If you want to shorten the script, copy your part of it and do not copy what the seller might answer. Add actual answers later so you can practice your responses and become an **expert in answering objections.**

Most Common Objections

1. I want to save money by not paying a commission.
2. I had a bad experience with an agent.
3. I do not want to be tied to a contract; I do not want to sign any contracts.
4. What if the realtor does nothing to sell it?
5. I would prefer to sell it myself.
6. My spouse does not want to work with a realtor.
7. I will only pay if there is a buyer.
8. I do not want to work with realtors.

Response to Objections

1. **I want to save money by not paying a commission:**

   Do you think that you are going to save money by not having an agent who represents you?
   Them: _____
   If I can show you how working with me, with me representing you, you will come out with the same amount of money or more than without my representation, would you work with me?
   Them: _____

2. **I had a bad experience with an agent.**

   What did this agent do wrong that you didn't like?
   Them: _____
   I understand. What do you think this agent should have done to make it a better fit?

Them: _____

My way of working is ...., my specialty is......,

Listen to the seller and tailor your response so you know what they need to hear about who their ideal agent is and how their ideal agent will work for their benefit. It helps to use similar words as the seller uses to build trust.

Hearing the seller is a key element to close the deal. If the seller wanted the agent to do an open house, you must do at least one if you want to get the listing. Never say you will do something if you don't plan on doing it.

3. **I do not want to be tied to a contract; I do not want to sign any contracts.**

    I understand, and I don't like contracts either. For this reason, I created a contract that is easy to get out of. You can cancel at no cost, even the next day if you want. It is an easy exit. Just fire me. If I give you all the conditions you want and the assurance that you can cancel at any time you want, is this something that would catch your attention, and could we work together?

    Them: _____

    Also explain that the agreement is a work agreement that the state requires when an agent represents a seller. A written agreement is in their favor, since you will both have what they want in writing.

4. **What if the realtor does nothing to sell it?**

    I guarantee you I will put my best effort into selling your home. If you allow me to meet with you, I can show you the marketing plan that I have specially designed for your property.

    If the owner lives in another city, you can do a meeting through Zoom or Google Meet. Remember, you should already have your marketing plan, list of websites, and other information ready to send to potential clients on your computer.

    When do you think would be a good time to show you the marketing plan, during the week or the weekend?

    Them: _____

5. **I would prefer to sell it myself.**

    Can I ask you why you want to sell it yourself?

    Them: _____

If their answer is to save the commission, answer objection #1 above and ask for the appointment.

If they do not give you an appointment, offer them the option that both of you can sell it, but that you have an exclusivity for all agents. They can sign the listing agreement and sell it on their own to anyone who is not represented by an agent, and if the buyer is not an agent. Explain that you have access to the MLS, which will improve their visibility regardless of who sells the house. You will need to explain all these details in person instead of over the phone since you will need to put it in writing.

6. **My spouse does not want to work with a realtor.**

   Could I ask why your spouse does not want to work with an agent?
   Them: _____

   Depending on what the answer is, tell them something to get the appointment. You could tell them you'll call in a day or two to talk to the spouse and maybe they'll change their mind, or it could be the person you're talking to on the phone will try to convince them for you.

7. **I will only pay if there is a buyer.**

   Perfect, could I come by tomorrow or the day after to see the property, so I can better talk about your property to my buyers?

8. **I do not want to work with realtors.**

   Could I ask you Mr. Seller why you do not want to be represented? Have you had bad experiences with any agents in the past?
   You may get other objections, but always try to answer with a question to get to the root of the problem and get the appointment. Use several ways to persuade them.

Script: Calling Expired Listings

Example #1

You: Hello *Seller*, my name is _____ with ABC Realty. I wanted to know if you are still selling your property.

Them: Yes.

You: Would you cooperate with an agent if I bring you a qualified buyer?

Them: If you have a buyer, yes.

You: Perfect, which day is better to see your house, tomorrow or Saturday?

Them: I do not know if I can. I am busy.

You: It will not take much time, and it is without any commitment since I will be in the area showing other properties to some of my buyers and I want to get the opportunity to know more about your property

Them: Ok, Saturday is fine.

You: In the afternoon or night?

Them: _____

You: Excellent. At 3 or 5?

Them: 3:00 pm.

You: See you soon and thank you.

If they say they're no longer selling the house.

Them: No.

You: Then you already sold your house?

Them: No.

You: Do you plan to sell your house later?

Them: Yes.

You: When?

Them: In about 6 months.

You: Very well, do you have an agent that you will work with or are already interviewing some?

Them: No.

You: I would like you to give me the opportunity to show you my marketing plan for your property without any commitment. Do you think I could drop by your house tomorrow or Saturday?

Them: I am not too sure.

You: Once you sell your house where you plan to move?

Them: Orlando. I already bought a house in Orlando. We are in it.

You: How long do you have to move?

Them: Between 3 to 6 months.

You: (Seller name) _____, you probably want to sell before buying and I would love to stop by your house once again since I work in your area, and my team and I have several buyers. Do you think it is better tomorrow or Friday afternoon?

Them: Friday at 6:00 pm

You: Great! I will be there

Example of Expired #2

You: Hello, seller, it's _____, from ABC Realty. I specialize in properties that have been for sale and for some reason could not be sold. In my records I see that you had your house for sale. Are you still interested in selling your house?

Them: Yes _____ No _____

You: Only last month my team and I sold almost all our own listings because we dedicated ourselves to moving our own inventory. If you are still interested in selling your property, I would love to meet with you and sell your home. Which day is best for you during the week or weekend?

Them: _____

*Continue until they give you the appointment. If they have objections, persist until you get the appointment. Remember, you are deaf to **NO** answers. Ask another question and then try again to get the appointment.

Example #3: Expired Listings

You: Hi, I am _____, with _____. I see your property listing expired. Do you still want to sell?

Them: Yes.

You: Have you interviewed other agents to represent you with the sale of your house?

Them: Yes/no.

You: Well, do you know why your house was not sold?

Them: No.

You: Are you familiar with the marketing plan I use for sellers who had their home for sale and could not sell it?

Them: No.

You: I would love to show it to you without any commitment. Would Tuesday morning or Wednesday be better after 6:00 pm?

Them: Wednesday.

You: Fantastic, I will see you Wednesday at 6:00 pm. Thank you.

Script: Calling Sellers by Referral

You: Hello, _____, my name is _____. You do not know me, but your name was given to me by a friend of both _____. They told me to call you.

You: (Friend name) told me I could help you with the sale of your home because you are thinking of selling your property. They told me to call you because they want you to be in good hands. That's the reason I am calling you. When are you thinking about moving?

Them: _____

You: Have you made any agreements with any agents?

Them: Yes _____ No _____

You: You have not signed anything yet? The best thing to do is for me to come see your property since I have clients looking in your area. I would like to see it before showing it to them.

You: Do you think it is better on Tuesday or Thursday?

Them: _____

You: Excellent!

Continue giving them options until you get the appointment. If it gets difficult, tell them your meeting is without any commitment, and you will bring them a complimentary market study and a gift such as a Starbucks card ($5-$10). The thought of bringing a small gift is more important than the amount; do not go overboard.

Script: Calling Properties in Foreclosure

You: Good morning/afternoon/evening Mr./Mrs. Owner, my name is _____, with Your Realty. The reason for my call is, based on our records, your property is registered in foreclosure (or pre-foreclosure). I want to offer you my free services and find out what you want to do with your property, so I can help.

You: Do you want to extend your stay at the property, sell it, modify your loan, or let the bank take away your house?

Them: _____

If they want to sell the property, continue with the call, and set up an appointment.

You: Which day would be more convenient to speak in person (in this case it's better to talk in person), during the week or weekend?

Them: _____

You: Perfect. I will see you on _____. Do you live in the house?

Them: Yes _____ No _____

Cold Calls, Warm Calls, and Hot Calls

Refer to Chapter 1 for these scripts.

Best Hours to Call

The best hours to call are from 9:00 am-11:00 am and in the afternoon any time from 4:00 pm until 8:45 pm. It's most important to call in the time *you* have free because people put their cell phone on silent and few people have a home phone.

If the only free time you can spare for calls is over your lunch hour and you dedicate 30 minutes to an hour to calling prospects, do it. This is also a good time for potential clients because many take their lunch hour to return calls and take care of personal business.

Farming

Farming is a system or marketing plan that is concentrated and limited to a specific area. Just like a farmer grows his crops and sees the fruit of his labor, you should be patient and invest the time it will take to see success. Assume this strategy will take at least six months to a year and be consistent.

An ideal way to farm the market is to choose an area that you like for some specific reason, an area where your office is located, or where you live. It will be easier for you to go to appointments or get acquainted with potential clients because they are your neighbors.

When you are considering a specific area, research it to find out the percentage that list compared to the percentage that sells. Do the sales happen quickly? Is there a dominant agent already working in the area? All the information you need about the area can be found on the MLS.

How will you know the return and if it suits you? Go into the MLS and find out how many properties are there and how many have sold. The more movement, the better. Compare several subdivisions to choose the one with the highest percentage in relation to sales. If it is very low, you should not invest it this area. Keep looking until you find one with a better return.

The percentage must be more than 11%. How does this work?

> Example:
> In a subdivision of 600 houses, 78 sold.
> 78 sold/600 houses = 13%.
> This subdivision is fine to choose, since it has a percentage of more than 11%; otherwise, the money and effort in seeing the results will take a long time.

When choosing an area, some agents focus on areas with medium to high prices to compensate for the investment they will make to sell a property.

To find if there is a dominant agent already working in the area, check each listing in the subdivision to find out if the same agent is repeated. If you find various agents, you can pick your area to focus on and begin to position yourself as a specialist in the area.

If you want to investigate more, visit with FSBO listings under the pretext of finding out how their area moves. You will gain valuable information and potentially pick up new clients.

Direct Mail

It will be cheaper to send mail via direct mail than to send it yourself using the post office. You can find direct mail services in places like UPS retail locations or mail stores. Google "direct mail," then choose the closest location. Be consistent and send a mailer to your target market every month.

Postcards

Sending postcards is cheaper than letters. To have the best results, choose your postcard design wisely. Design several, starting from a template, then change it each time so you don't bore your client base. There are platforms online such as Top Producer, and others that will do this for you, built for real estate agents. Also, printing companies such as Vista Print and Canva will print and mail the postcard for you.

Example:

I will sell your house in 90 days or you don't pay me anything!

Satisfaction Guaranteed

Your Name
305-444-4444
www.yourname.com

Place your name and contact information on either side of the postcard, whichever you prefer.

To offer this program you must explain that the property must be at the price you designate. The seller must also agree to collaborate with you in everything such as appointments and open houses. The price must be in line with the condition of the property. For example, a property in excellent condition will sell at a certain price in a specific market, no more and no less. If they want to sell it for more, tell them they can, but if it is not sold in 90 days, they must understand *they* chose the price not you. The 90-day guarantee would not apply in that case. If they use the price you advise, you will stick by your 90-day sales guarantee.

If you feel sure that even if they set the price, you can still sell it (since you have a client who is interested in the property, the area is excellent either to sell or get customers by the yard sign, or you feel safe), making the guarantee is your decision. Even if a low offer comes in, the sellers could still accept the offer.

If the property is in below-standard condition, you must lower the price compared to other property values in the area. The seller can either fix up the property or lower the price.

Example #2

Offer a certificate for $500.00 off repairs to be done by a contractor from a list you provide. The contractors will deduct the $500 from the cost of the job. The coupon could be printed with the name of the contractor/handyman or just give your client the list and they can call someone on it, depending on what they need. Contact several companies and tell them about your coupon. This will help them grow their business, and they could sponsor part or all of the $500.00 discount.

$500.00
For Repairs

Dear Customer:

Thank you for choosing me as your preferred agent. To show my gratitude for working with me, you have earned $500.00 for the repair of your home. This will help me sell your property faster and at a better price.

I will give you a list of contractors to choose from and they will discount your repairs cost by $500.00.

Property address:

Certificate #000128

_____

Ivania Alvarado

Website

You can get a free website from your board of realtors or from your broker. You could also create one yourself from different **website builders:**

- Wix—**Best** All-Around **Website Builder**.
- Weebly—Ideal for Small Businesses.
- SITE123—**Great** Design Assistance.
- Strikingly—Made for Simple **Websites**.
- WordPress—**Perfect** for Blogging.
- Jimdo—Small Online Store **Builder**.
- Simple Site—**Great** Mobile Editor.

Another option is to hire a website developer who specializes in real estate web services, to help you with your branding, image, and promotion. It is highly recommended for all agents to have a personalized website for all their information and listings. If you can invest a little more, you could buy templates to create a website for each property. Your clients will help you in the sale when they see their house with their own website, and they can direct their friends to it and share the link. This is a great way to get more customers interested in working with you.

Blogs

Having a real estate blog will keep your customers informed and provides a database where you can store contact information. The good thing is that blogs are free.

You must create your own categories and articles for your blog. You can also copy and paste information from various real estate websites such as Houselogic.com and Realtor.org. Your board of realtors will have connections with several websites containing great information for your audience. Have your national association number ready in case some of these websites ask you for it before copying and pasting their information.

Places to create your blog: Active Rain, WordPress, and RAMB blog (for members only).

Social Media

See Chapter 1 for more information about creating and maintaining your social media presence.

Offers, Gifts, Discounts, Incentives...

Be creative and come up with a variety of incentives so you and your customers don't get bored. You always want to have something new and fun to offer your customers.

Offer a free inspection if they buy from you that is refunded at the time of closing (POC means paid out at closing). The customer will get a credit at closing that is deducted from their closing cost.

Give away little gifts like Starbucks gift cards of $5 - $10 to sellers as a thank you for giving you an appointment. The amount is not as important as the intention. They will remember how you appreciated the opportunity to discuss business with you. You could send the gift card by mail, thanking them for giving you the opportunity, so you have more chances of getting the listing in case they are still thinking about which agent to use.

You can offer a percentage discount on repairs such as painting from someone you refer to your client from your list of contractors. When you send them a customer, they will give them a percentage discount, either on everything or on something specific.

If the prospect buys, sells, or rents with you, you can offer a certificate that entitles them to receive a credit at the time of closing. Contact a few title companies and ask them to provide gift certificates to your clients to use at closing such as a discount on their title policy or a free processing fee. You can give the certificate at your listing presentation which will differentiate you from the rest of the agents your prospect might consider.

$350.00 Coupon for Preferred Customer

The holder of this coupon is entitled to a reduction of $350.00 on the purchase or sale of their home.

Given the _____ month _____ of 20_____

_____, Expires _____

Your Name, Broker Associate

Name of your company, address, and phone

Note: This certificate *is* transferable to family members and friends.

Valued Customer
$1,000.00

Dear (customer name)_____ **Date:** _____

This certificate is valid up to 3 years from today.

I appreciate your business and the trust you place in me. As a valued customer, I want to give you a certificate valued at $1,000.00 for your next sale or purchase using my real estate services. You can use this certificate at closing. This my way of saying thank you.

Property:

#0024 Certificate

Your Name:

Broker:

Chapter 3

Renters and Landlords

Working with Tenants

One good thing about working with tenants is that it is fast income. When you specialize in it and perfect your process, you always have one check coming in after another. Be sure to prequalify them in advance so as not to waste your time.

How to Find Tenants

Getting tenants is very easy. Just put some advertisements out about a property in the area and the monthly price, and you will have a deluge of clients. Have your checklist handy and send each tenant the questionnaire. Only work with the ones who send the questionnaire and their complete information back to you.

You will always be busy with tenants but work smart. Do not go into overdrive with the first tenant who calls you. Only show properties to prequalified tenants. Set your conditions and respect yourself, your work, your money, and your time, and you will see how everything flows better in your favor.

Avenues you can use to place your ads: Facebook, Twitter, LinkedIn, YouTube, WhatsApp, QQ, Q Zone, WeChat, Instagram, Weibo, Google AdWords, Snapchat, Pinterest, Craigslist, and more.

Prequalifying the Tenant

Prequalifying will save you time and money. When you talk with them on the phone, always ask as much information as possible. Have a checklist available so you can ask everything you need to know before you agree to work with the client.

Keep the checklist on your computer and on your cell phone to send it to them via email and text message.

When you see them, you will already have all their information, which is also helpful for security reasons when it's time to show properties.

Questions to Ask the Tenant

- Full name as it appears on their driver's license. (At the time of closing this property or applying to the association, the contract must be in the same name that appears on the license).
- Driver's license or any legal U.S. ID. Ask them to send you a copy.
- Their current home address.
- Phone numbers
- How much money do they make per year?
- W-2
- Credit report
- Background check
- Email address
- How much cash do they have on hand?
- Do they have the first month's deposit and last month's rent?
- How many people will live on the property and what are the relationships among them?
- How many are over the age of 18?
- What kind of property are they looking for?
- How many rooms and bathrooms?
- Do they have a pet? YES _____ NO _____ What type of pet? _____ Breed? _____ How much does it weigh? _____
- Do they have a commercial truck that can't be parked in a residential area, or do they have somewhere else to park it?

Questions necessary to be able to rent with associations or that some owners require:

- Have you ever been evicted?
- Have you had any felonies?
- Have you ever gone bankrupt?
- How is your credit?

Tenant Application

Tenant Name 1: _____ Telephone _____

Date of Birth: _____ DL# _____ SS# _____

Tenant Name 2: _____ Telephone _____

Date of Birth: _____ DL# _____ SS# _____

Residential History for the Last 2 Years

Address Present Tenant 1:_____

Date you moved in: _____ Date you left: _____

Owner Name: _____ Tel: _____ Rent $ _____

Reason for move: _____

Previous Address: _____

Time of Residence: _____

Have you and/or Co-applicant ever been evicted? Yes _____ NO _____
If the answer is yes, explain _____

Have you had a bankruptcy? _____ Date? _____

Address Present Tenant 2:_____

Date you moved in: _____ Date you left: _____

Owner Name: _____ Tel: _____ Rent $ _____

Reason for move: _____

Previous Address: _____

Time of Residence: _____

Have you and/or Co-applicant ever been evicted? Yes _____ NO _____
If the answer is yes, explain _____

Have you had a bankruptcy? _____ Date? _____

Automobile Information

Tag: _____ Plate# _____ Model _____

Tag: _____ Plate# _____ Model _____

In Case of an Emergency

Name: _____ Relation: _____ Phone: _____

Address: _____

Name: _____ Relation: _____ Phone: _____

Address: _____

Name: _____ Relation: _____ Phone: _____

Address: _____

Employment History

Company Applicant 1: _____ Supervisor: _____

Address: _____ Phone: _____

Start Date: _____ Position: _____ Gross weekly salary $ _____

Company Applicant 2: _____ Supervisor: _____

Address: _____ Phone: _____

Start Date: _____ Position: _____ Gross weekly salary $ _____

Banking References/Optional

Bank: _____ Account# _____

Bank: _____ Account# _____

Personal References

Name: _____ Relationship: _____ Telephone: _____

Name: _____ Relationship: _____ Telephone: _____

Name: _____ Relationship: _____ Telephone: _____

Name: _____ Relationship: _____ Telephone: _____

_____,I authorize and give the right to verify by reason, the application including but not limited to credit check, criminal history, eviction civil records, owner verification, work verification; and exercise in its sole discretion to the extent so to reject this application and/or cancel any lease agreement that may be entered into between the parties pursuant to this application, whether during the term of such lease and/or any extension or renewal thereof, if the applicant has made any false statements or falsehoods in the application. Furthermore, the applicant(s) certify that it has not omitted any information from this application, in addition to any documents in the application package, exhibitions and/or annexes. I also grant the Real Estate company (add real estate company name) to investigate all information provided in this application. All relevant data found during this may be disclosed to the association and/or owner is authorized to obtain a credit report through a credit reporting agency of your choice.

Applicant's Signature: _____ Date: _____

Co-applicant's Signature: _____ Date: _____

Script: Potential Tenants Who Were Referred to You

Example of calling a referral, warm call:

Hello, this is _____. How are you? Your friend _____ gave me your phone as they told me you are interested in renting a home. Is that correct? (Listen, do not talk.)

Perfect, what area would you like to live in? (Listen.)

How many bedrooms and bathrooms are you looking for? (Listen.)

Excellent, and how much rent are you willing to pay monthly?

All right, how much are you currently paying? (Listen.)

I see. Do you have the three months that are required to rent which is the first month, last month, and security deposit? (Listen.)

Good. I will send you by text or email a questionnaire for you to fill it out. Please respond each question and then send it back to me.

I will be looking for the properties you told me to look for while you do the questions. Which day would be better for you to see the properties, something during the week or on the weekend?

Perfect, in the morning or in the afternoon?

Excellent! Is this the best phone number to use? What email address would you like me to use to send the questionnaire?

Thank you very much. See you tomorrow at (at the time and day you have agreed).

Script: Contacting a Landlord

You: Hi, I am _____, with _____. I noticed that you are renting your property, is this correct?

Them: Yes _____ No _____

You: How soon do you want to rent your property?

You: I would love to see your property inside as I work in your area and have qualified tenants in that price range who might be interested.

You: Would Thursday afternoon or Saturday morning be better for you?

You: Around 11:00 am?

Continue until they give you the appointment.

If they say no, try to ask another question:

You: Where do you plan to move? or Do you have another property in addition to this where you live? or Do you have other properties that need to be rented right now or soon?

You can ask if they have other properties either for rent or sale that they could give you to list.

Specializing in working with landlords is a great way to create a monthly income stream because landlords usually have more than one property and they buy and sell properties too.

Script: Landlords Who Were Referred to You

You: Hello, _____, my name is _____. You do not know me, but your name was given to me by a friend of both _____. They told me to call you.

You: _____ told me I could help you find a qualified and responsible tenant as you are thinking of putting your property up for rent. They told me to call you, as they want you to be in good hands.

You: When are you thinking about renting your property?

Them: _____

You: Have you made any agreements with any agents?

Them: Yes _____ No _____

You: Have you signed anything?

You: The best thing to do is for me to come to see your property. I have clients in the area, and I would like to see it before showing them. Which would be better, Tuesday or Thursday?

Them: _____

You: Excellent!

Continue giving them options until you get the appointment. If they push back, let them know meeting with you is without any commitment or obligation. Bring a gift card such as a Starbucks card of $5-$10 with you to your first meeting. The exact amount you give is less important than the gift itself.

Finally, offer them the easy exit: "If necessary, fire me."

Working with the Landlord/Owner

Working with the owner of a home is an excellent way of generating recurring monthly income if you add this provision to the rental agreement.

When you hold these contracts, be sure to call the tenant 60 days in advance of the contract expiring to see if they want to continue with the rental agreement. Your options would be to write up a new contract if they want to stay or to put it back on the market if they want to move.

If the tenant does not wish to renew the lease, you must coordinate with them when you show the property to potential new tenants. Be sure to write this on the lease. If the tenant does not renew, the tenant must allow the owner or owner agent to get access to the property to show the property to new tenants.

The renewal fee could be at the same term (10% per month) or a month of rent, either for the listing agent or for both agents. It also could be for a lower fee.

Also, when you list the property on the MLS, indicate whether the contract is renewable and whether it will be under the same terms, a lower commission, or no commission on renewals.

Telemarketing

See chapter 1 for more information about telemarketing.

How to Find Landlords

You decide if you want to buy a leads list of landlords and save time. Otherwise, you can do all the research through the MLS, IMAPP, tax rolls, public records, newspapers, online advertisements, Craigslist, and others. These are some of the most common methods and are available to you at no additional cost. You will just need to invest time to do your research.

Redx

List of customers that you can purchase monthly, quarterly, semi-annually, or annually. The list is organized by type of client: FSBO (for sale by owner), expired listings, FRBO (for rent by owner), and foreclosure. Every list has a price, and you buy them by county or area code.

Bressers

Bressers provides lists of databases and directories to identify renters, landlords, homeowners, owners, and more. It includes the zip code and address to help you create marketing plans.

Zbuyer

They create a budget base of how much you want to invest per month and sell each lead individually. The leads are shared less often among other agents compared to other services, but they are more expensive.

FSBO Magazines, Newspapers, Websites, Lists, Craigslist, etc.

You can find listings on the internet, and in shops, supermarkets, and more.

Presentation to the Landlord

See Chapter 2 for more information about listing presentations.

The presentation is the same whether you are talking to a seller or a landlord. The difference for landlords is that the comparables are based on rents not sales. You must use comparables within a period of three to six months for rented, actives, and pendings.

Website to Attract Landlords

Just like you would make a website to attract traffic for buyers or sellers, you'll want to create a website to attract landlords. When you create it, determine your specialty and who you want to attract. Mention things relating to managing rentals, listing for rent, and important information that will interest the landlord such as evictions, notices, tenant screening, etc.

Offers, Discounts, and Gifts

See chapter II and adapt your promotions for landlords by offering less money since you earn less in commissions. Talk to moving companies and people who do repairs for whomever your client is and offer something they can use now or in the future.

Ask yourself these important questions when crafting promotions:

- What is my goal?
- Have I caught their attention?
- Are they responding? Why? And why not?

And most importantly:

- What is the benefit to them?

Let clients know the benefits they will receive when working with you. When a client sees how they are benefiting, that will help you close a listing transaction. Use this powerful tool.

Preferred Customer

Dear Customer

Receive a 20% discount with moving company ABC as a token of appreciation for your business. Thank you!

Realtor: _____

Date: _____

This certificate is valid for 3 years from the issue date above and is transferable only to a family member and/or friends.

Chapter 4

Delegating

Delegating is extremely important if you want to grow. When you delegate, you can multiply your income, clients, and listings. The key is in knowing who to hire. You must have patience when you choose who you hire and be quick when it is necessary to fire someone. If you do not, you can lose not only customers but even the business.

You must train them, even if the person is well-qualified.

Your First Assistant

One of the most common mistakes is to hire your spouse as your assistant. Unless they are good for the job and like the business, firing them could become a problem in your marriage. If you do hire your spouse, ask some questions before to know if they like doing the job. The best option would be for them to get a real estate license. Then you could both hire an assistant together. At least if they have a license, if you decide to hire your spouse, as a licensed agent they will be able to do more things in your business. Your spouse could show your listings, or you could divide the work into specializations. You could do listing presentations and they could work with buyers or tenants.

An assistant may or may not be licensed, depending on what you need. At first you may not need the assistant to be licensed, but you do need them to be tech-trained, polite and courteous with clients, a quick learner, and be able to do many things at once. If you work with bilingual clients, another useful skill is for them to speak two languages. Be sure to pay your assistant well or you will lose them.

Duplicate

You achieve duplication when you have your first assistant. Your next step is your first partner, and so on as you multiply your efforts and results.

Hire the Perfect Team

Having the perfect team is essential as you reach higher and higher levels of success. For example, if you want to dedicate yourself to sellers, your team must include an agent specialized in buyers, then in tenants and so on. As you expand, another agent could help with listings in general (for sale or for rent, sellers, or landlords). At least one person on your team needs to know how to do videos, manage a YouTube channel, and post on social media. Social media outlets are the new way of selling and promoting real estate.

Multiply

Multiplication is when you have a team of two or more agents and one or two assistants running. This will multiply your production and income at least three to four times more than what you closed previously.

Having a team is ideal because if you have ads you will always have someone answering the phone. When you get a referral, they will be taken care of immediately. If a customer calls last minute to see a listing or a specific property, anyone can go as they can split the work and take turns on last minute calls. They can alternate weekends, so you have a weekend off sometimes.

Your team is your strength and will translate into more customers and better service.

Refer Part of Your Business

It is necessary to refer your prospects who are not the customers you want to attract to other agents. They can still represent income. If you want to specialize in a type of client or an area and you do not have a partner to share customers, you should refer all these clients to other agents. If you don't, that will take up the time you can dedicate to your target clients. For example, if you are the listing agent of an apartment for rent and many prospective tenants call you, you could give these referrals to another agent for a 20-25% referral fee. You can still focus on your target client type, listings, and at the same time get a referral fee.

If you do not have a team, it is good to refer clients to other agents. At the same time, this can be a way to create a team with a plan to refer your business to your team. If you get a lot of business to refer, it would be nice to have a part-time or full-time assistant to record it, or you do it yourself.

Chapter 5

Selling Through Zoom and Google Meet

Virtual selling is a great tool that started before Covid-19, but many people did not use it because they preferred in-person contact. Now that we've experienced the pandemic, most sales and jobs are hybrid and others are fully virtual. These are some of the virtual platforms that are helpful to perform any real estate transaction: Zoom, Microsoft Teams, Google Meet, Join.me, Whereby, and Orbits.

Real estate is not the exception to the rule. We can now see more clients through virtual meetings such as Zoom, Google Meet, and other virtual platforms.

Advantages of Selling Real Estate Through a Virtual Platform

- You can see and handle more clients in less time.
- You can work from home.
- You can have more time with your family.
- If your client does not come, you did not lose any time in the office waiting for them, driving to the office, or money on gas.
- It's great for choosing the properties they're interested in when doing the first search, as well as saving the properties and synchronizing the automatic email service for them.
- They see market prices, and it becomes easier to choose the properties they like because you are choosing the properties together.

- They can share their documents with you relating to the transaction such as the credit report, income statement, and prequalification letter to make sure they have everything you need before you start working.
- You can have other people join the meeting for their prequalification such as the loan originator, another agent, your assistant, or your broker.
- You and your client can be anywhere and meet at the same time even on vacation.
- It's great when there are several people in the transaction like the husband, wife, and older children who want to participate in the buying process, especially when all the clients cannot be together but can be online at the same time.
- It's good for clients outside your area, city, state, or in another country.
- It's good to use in combination with your open house for people who cannot come. It will expand your potential client base.
- It can be used for showing properties.
- It can be used for a listing presentation and to show your marketing plan and the competition in the area for all the other properties that are for sale, sold, pending, etc.
- You can explain anything they did not understand about the contract. It's easier to address it directly.
- You can fill or prefill a contract with them to explain the most important topics.
- Many more advantages!

Learn to Work Hybrid and/or Remote as a Real Estate Agent or Broker

The advantage of this wonderful career is that you decide how you want to work. You can be hybrid and/or remote. In my opinion hybrid is the best for any real estate agent. Real estate is a profession that is constantly changing and improving. Whether we like it or not, we must improve and go with the flow. The pandemic forced all of us to use virtual platforms that can make our job easier, and we should all learn about them. Some agents still need to adapt to it, while others need to learn how to use it to provide better service to their clients. After you learn how to work and close a virtual deal, you will love it too.

You can use Google Meet if you have a Google (Gmail) account. Go to Google.com, then click on the nine dots to the left of your profile picture (your profile picture might show up as the first letter of your name instead). That will pull up Google apps. Choose the calendar. When the calendar is open, click the + sign where it says Create and click on the drop-down arrow. Click Event and fill out the title. Click next to the clock to choose the date and time of your meeting. Follow all the instructions and do not forget to add your guest names (the system will have all your Google contacts). Add Google Meet video conference and save.

On the meeting date and time, go to your calendar, click on the meeting, then click Join Now. You will be the presenter. Have your browser open and ready before you start the meeting with your client, so you don't waste time. You want to show that you're professional and know what you are doing.

Have the MLS website pulled up and log into it with your credentials, then prepare the MLS search from the perspective of a seller or buyer. Have the contract and your presentation or the Power-Point you will review with the buyer open. Think of everything you might need for your meeting and have it ready.

You can use Google Meet, Zoom, or other virtual platforms on your computer and cell phone. If you use Google Meet on your cell phone, go to your email account and on the right bottom corner, you will see the word "Meet" with their symbol. Click there and join with a code or start a new meeting.

For a new meeting, you can get the link to share, start an instant meeting, or schedule it in Google Calendar. A cell phone is great for doing open houses or showing a house to a client who can't come to see the property in person. You can share the link through WhatsApp, email, and social media.

Zoom is similar. You will need to download Zoom on your computer in advance and be sure to check the audio settings before you are with your client. I recommend downloading Zoom on your cell phone too. When you download Zoom, it is easy. Just click Zoom, then click on meeting to schedule a meeting with the + sign. Schedule the meeting by filling in the starting date, duration, and more. Remember to save it.

You can schedule your meeting using Outlook, Google Calendar, or any other calendar. I recommend you schedule your meetings in Google Calendar because it is easy to add guests and send the invitation. Another way to do it is by copying the invitation link and sending the link to your clients. You can do this through Outlook, Google Calendar, Yahoo, etc.

When you start the meeting, you can invite people from there. While the meeting is in progress, under participant, click invite. It will open your contacts and your email account. Choose email and invite your clients. Another way to do this is as soon as you open Zoom, click on new meeting, and invite the clients.

Quick Way to Start Zoom:

- Start at Zoom's signup page.
- Activate your account.
- Create your account name and password.
- You can invite colleagues or clients if you wish.
- Try doing a test meeting first.
- After you have installed the Zoom app, you will see buttons to "Join a Meeting" or "Sign In."
- Sign into the app.
- Now you are ready to Zoom with your client.
- Choose a professional picture in case one day you are not joining with video and a nice background that relates to your real estate career.

BASIC Zoom for Personal meetings is free. You can host up to 100 participants for up to 40 minutes and it has unlimited one-on-one meetings with a 30-hour time limit per meeting.

How to Use Google Meet:

- Go to meet.google.com (or open the app on iOS or Android or start a meeting from Google Calendar).
- Click Start new meeting or enter your meeting code.
- Choose the Google account you want to use.
- Click Join meeting.
- You will have the ability to add others to your meeting, too.

Google Meet is free for users on a 1-to-1 video chats for 24 hours, and group calls are capped at 100 participants with a 60-minute duration. At 55 minutes, you'll get a warning message.

First Virtual Interview with a Buyer or Tenant

The first meeting is one of the most important meetings. You will create rapport, the link between you and your clients. Some agents skip this first appointment because they consider it just more time spent with a client. I consider it the best investment time I can have with a client.

Why? It has many advantages: You do not lose your value time with a client who is not ready, willing, and able. A customer could *want* to buy, but that does not mean they are ready to buy or to buy in the way you and your company allow. They may also want concessions the market is not prepared to deliver.

Example: A person wants to buy, but they ask for a 10% discount on a property when we're in a seller's market. This first appointment will help you educate your client about the market you are in now. It's likely they will lose out on the offer because there are not enough properties for sale compared to the number of buyers who want to buy. This meeting is all about setting expectations, not just to prequalify the buyer. It is also to explain how you work and how everything will proceed when you find the right property for them.

The first interview can be in person, over the phone, or virtual. We are going to discuss the virtual presentation in this chapter.

Set up the Zoom or Google Meet link invitation and send it to all the participants. Include only the people who will make decisions on the buying or renting process.

Try to do a concise meeting and get everything you need before you start: the contract that you will use, the MLS page is open, etc. Remind the client to have all the documents you asked them to email back to you before the meeting so you can explain their qualification or any issue to be solved in the meeting. If necessary, you can invite other people like your broker, team member, or loan originator.

Do not do the meeting if your client did not provide all the documents you requested. It is better to reschedule when they have everything.

The day of the meeting, always enter before the scheduled time in case your clients enter before you. Like any other appointment, be sure to remind them about the meeting.

- Dress professionally, at least from your torso to the top of your face.
- Accept each participant who is in the waiting room when the admit button appears.
- Start greeting them one by one.
- Break the ice and ask about them, how they are feeling, why they want to buy or rent, the area they are interested in, and so on to know more about them and what they want.
- Ask about something you need, or you tell them about the credit report if they are a tenant. Example: "You have a great credit report, and your wife does too. Before the lease expires, you should consider buying."
- After everybody is in the meeting and you create rapport, talk about any important areas in their documents.

If they do not qualify, you should not have this meeting. Instead, call and tell them they do not qualify for what they want unless the price and terms can be adjusted, or they find a cosigner.

Let's say this is a buyer:

You: Mr. and Mrs. Buyer, based on your prequalification letter you qualify for a $450,000 house. Is that the price at which you both want to buy?

Them: Yes

You: Perfect. Let's start looking at properties. I already started a search and I want to show both of you the properties and know if you both like them. Or we can adjust the search criteria of the property such as the location, type of property, rooms, price, and more. Any questions before I proceed?

If they like all the properties you show them, save all the properties, create a new contact, and create an auto email, so they start receiving emails about any new listing in the desired area. If they did not like the search results, change the criteria together with your buyer until everyone is happy with the results.

Schedule the first showing date and time while you are with them if any of the properties are on lockbox status. You can schedule appointments for the rest of the properties after you finish the meeting.

Explain how the market is performing and how you work:

You: Mr. and Mrs. Buyer, as you can see the inventory is low for the types of properties both of you like, so when we see these three properties, if both of you like one of the properties, we must act immediately, or we could lose it. The way the market is performing right now, buyers are not usually asking for price discounts or any other type of help. If you like a house and you want it, to get the house, you must be ready to compete with other buyers. Ok?

You: Perfect. Any questions?

You: Thanks, Mr. and Mrs. Buyer. I will see you _____ at _____. Goodbye.

First Virtual Interview with a Seller or Landlord

A virtual listing presentation is a great tool because you can show more comparables and other properties in the system. It is a great tool for sellers and landlords who live outside the area, in another state or country, or do not want to meet you in person for whatever reason.

Sellers expect more information from you than just suggesting a listing price for their property. When you are on your virtual listing presentation, educate your sellers and demonstrate your competence when it comes to marketing and selling their property.

Use the same protocol as the first interview above and have all the documents and presentations ready in advance, including the listing presentation, the CMA, IMAPP, RPR (use some of the pages), any comparables listed on your board's website, and the MLS page open. Always send a meeting reminder to the seller or landlord and all the clients involved in the transaction.

When you send the email reminder, have a generic template ready and fill in your client's name. Tell them how the presentation will be and what they can expect from you. Adjust the template to your style. If you are going to send a prelisting document, send the prelisting before this letter.

Sample Letter:

Dear Seller,

I am excited to meet you on _____ at _____ on Zoom/Google Meet. I will guide you through the step-by-step plan I use to get many homes **SOLD** in #_____ days or less.

The information I will share on the day of the listing presentation will include an overview of what it takes to sell your house in today's changing market.

When we meet virtually, we will look at current listings and determine a pricing strategy together. I will show you my marketing plan to sell your property for the fastest and highest price. Finally, you will be the one who chooses the best pricing strategy.

Sincerely,
Your Name
Company Name
Cell phone
Website

What to Have in Your Virtual Listing Presentation

Go to your local board website and find all the materials you need to do your marketing plan and presentation. For example, on the Miami Board of Realtors website go to:

Home » MIAMI Products & Services » Co-branded Marketing Materials.

You will find more than one hundred websites that will show your listing when you post it, including all the associations nationwide and internationally. There are 1.4 million active agents in the Board of Realtors in the U.S. This is an important marketing tool to show your sellers that demonstrates why working with you is so much better than trying to list the property without your help.

- Create a generic PowerPoint presentation you can reuse with other sellers and landlords. Your PowerPoint presentation can have slides only, audio and slides, or if you want, you can record yourself.
- Include at least one picture of their property to personalize your presentation.
- Your picture (professional).
- Your company logo.
- Talk about yourself (you can include your resume in the presentation).
- Talk about your company.
- Show the marketing techniques and campaigns you and your company use (list all the channels you will use to advertise their property: websites, magazines, blogs, social media,

real estate networks such as local, national, and international, open houses, door knocking, mail and email campaign, etc.).

- Explain to them that before their listings hit the MLS, you conduct a series of activities to generate buzz about their property and to make sure the home gets found online.
- Launch campaign. If you have a landing page for each listing, show this part; otherwise, do not mention it.
- A questionnaire that asks their desired price, showing times, if the property is vacant or occupied, association fees and time for acceptance, lockbox or electronic lockbox, and anything else related to the property. Make a generic questionnaire for all your transactions.
- Address the concern most sellers or landlords have about the time between the listing and closing.
- A slide that answers the question: Why work with me? List the advantages of working with you and what you will do for them. The seller cares about what you will do for them and for their property. Example: if you do open houses, send postcards in the neighborhood, knock on doors, or whatever else you do or will do.
- Explain the importance of pricing. Have a slide showing the disadvantages of listing an overpriced property. Explain the three types of pricing: the right price (it will sell the fastest at a better price and get bidding offers to get the highest and best terms with a few days on the market), slightly over price (some showings but no real offers with many days or months on the market with lower priced offers) and overpriced (no showings and no offers with many months on the market and the seller has to extend the contract or the listing becomes expired).
- Easy Exit Listing Agreement (only use this if your broker allows it). Explain that if they sign with you today, they can cancel any time with zero cancelation fees. This will help you get more listings.
- Listing agreement.
- Finally, talk about your commission.

Virtual Listing Presentation

- Start your Zoom or Google Meet full of energy and greet everyone as they arrive.
- Start breaking the ice and ask how they feel. Ask about their family and find some similarities with them to create a good connection.
- After you're all comfortable, start asking about the house. Find out where they are moving so you know why they are selling and how quickly they need to sell.

- Ask what they like the most about their house so you can use it as selling technique when you list it. Ask what they don't like about it, so you know about any problems you'll need to overcome in the selling process.
- Ask questions about the homeowner's association if any, showing instructions, the condition of the property, who lives in it, if is vacant or rented, etc.
- Start your PowerPoint presentation if you have prepared one. I recommend having one ready and following all the steps mentioned above. But if you do not have a PowerPoint presentation, have all the documents you will need already open on your computer and browser as mentioned in the list above.
- When you are finished with the first part of the presentation, you reach the most critical point: discussing the listing price and your commission. The goal is to get the listing. When the seller starts discussing the price and commission with you, it means they like you as an agent and the deal is almost done. You just need their signature.
- Have the pre-filled listing agreement open on your computer. Review it with them and discuss the price, the number of months in the listing agreement, and your commission. Send it to them while you are in the presentation. Approach the most important parts of the listing agreement. You're not there to do a listing agreement class, so be short and concise.
- Do not let the seller leave without negotiating the listing agreement. Ask them to sign there on their email, or if they say they will do it, ask them when to expect the agreement so you can start adding their listing to the MLS as a coming soon listing on the date they tell you. Tell them you will send the Coming Soon Status Seller Authorization Form to be signed by them.
- Immediately schedule an appointment to take pictures of the property, inspect the property, pick up keys, and install a lockbox. You can also include picking up the agreement in case they forget to send it back to you.

You: So, Mr. and Mrs. Seller, is it okay to come by tomorrow at noon or would the evening be better to take professional pictures?

Them: Oh, the house is not clean!

You: Don't worry. I can inspect the property and take some initial pictures, like the front of the house, the yard, and so on. Which is better, tomorrow or Wednesday?

You: Great, I will be there tomorrow, after 5 or 7 pm?

Thank them for the opportunity they gave you to give your presentation. Now you're finished!

Do not finish without the appointment. It is important to get the signed listing agreement, inspect the property, and take initial pictures of it so you can start the listing process.

As soon as you hang up with them, send a thank you card by mail. Get a gift card to any coffee place for $10 to show gratitude for their time. If you do not want to send a card, send a thank you letter or electronic postcard that you can do on Canva.com or a different graphics platform. Have a couple of nice designs you can reuse for all your clients. The day of the pictures and inspection, bring the gift card with you. This is not a requirement, but most sellers will appreciate it.

CANVA sample of email postcard:

If you send them the listing agreement and they want to review it with you or need help to open it, when you are in Zoom you can share your screen. Zoom also offers a feature where you can control the other participant's computer.

Important Slides for Your PowerPoint Presentation

The slides shown below are just examples. Create your own design and customize it to show your experience, personality, clientele, and company style. The importance of showing these slides is to provide inspiration for how to do your own. The first ones include the listing presentation, information about you, and client testimonials. You can use Canva.com to do your listing presentation. They have several samples. Another resource is Microsoft PowerPoint presentation software. You can use any other platform or combine several for the best results. Several slides are shown combined so there are fewer slides, but if you like, you can separate them into more slides.

123 Main Street, Miami, FL 33165
Mr. and Mrs. Seller
Listing Presentation & Marketing Plan

Presented by:
Your Name
Lic.#SL123467
Real Estate Agent
305-111-1111

YOUR REAL ESTATE COMPANY

Real estate listing presentation

by Your Name

APRIL 08, 2022

Your Real Estate Company

- In the industry since 2007
- Several active agents working as a team to sell all in-house listings.
- Our Broker has more than 26 years of experience
- Add the most important thing that your company has to offer

Your Name

- Licensed real estate broker since 1996
- Licensed real estate instructor
- Specializes in residential real estate
- Bachelor's degree in Supervision and Management-Accounting Concentration from Miami Dade College
- Master of Taxation in Florida Atlantic University
- Listing specialist
- Buyer Specialist
- List all designations you have.

Your Name

Licensed Real Estate Agent

REAL ESTATE LISTING — APRIL 2022

YEARS OF EXPERIENCE

Presentations are communication tools that can be used as demonstrations, lectures, speeches, reports, and more. It is mostly presented before an audience.

SPECIALIZATIONS

Presentations are communication tools that can be used as demonstrations, lectures, speeches, reports, and more. It is mostly presented before an audience.

OUR SATISFIED CLIENTS

Client Name

Accountant

Testimonials are short quotes from people who love your brand.

Client Name

Sales Manager

Testimonials are short quotes from people who love your brand.

Client Name

Chef

Testimonials are short quotes from people who love your brand.

Client Testimonials

Your Client Name

HOMEOWNER

Testimonials are short quotes from people who love your brand. It's a great way to convince customers to try your services.

Other Client Name

BUSINESS OWNER

Testimonials are short quotes from people who love your brand. It's a great way to convince customers to try your services.

Client Name

COMMERCIAL BUILDING OWNER

Testimonials are short quotes from people who love your brand. It's a great way to convince customers to try your services.

International Associations & agents all over the world

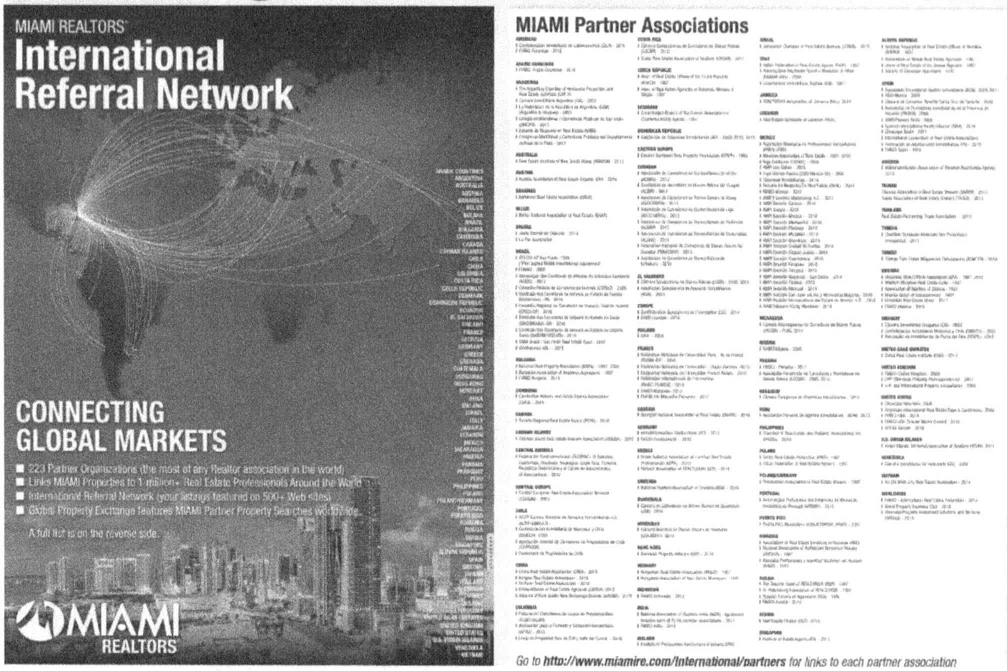

National Real Estate Network

Marketing Campaign & Advertising

- Over 700 local, national, and international websites: Realtor.com, Zillow.com, Truly.com, HotPads.com, RealEstate.com, Proxio.com, HomeFinder.com, Homes.com, RealtyTrac.com, HomesandLand.com, Foreclousure.com, Apartments.com, LandandFarm.com, LakehomesUSA.com, RiverhomesUSA.com, OceanhomesUSA.com, Close2Homes.com, Commercialsearch.realtor.com, ForRent.com, Homes2.me, IdealEstate.com, Houses.net, Miami.com, MiamiRealtors.com, Herald.com, Sucasa.com, RealtyStore.com, DreamHomeList.com, and hundreds more.
- 1.6 million realtors nationwide & millions of agents around the world
  - Most Social Media (Facebook, Instagram, Twitter, Pinterest, etc.)
  - Mail & email campaign
  - Open house, door knocking, etc.

Important questions to help me understand how to best serve YOU!

- Why are you selling?
- Where are you moving?
- How soon do you need to be there?
- What is your desired price?
- What are the best days and times to show the property?
- Is the property vacant or occupied?
- When does the lease expire? (If rented)
- What is the association fee and the time for acceptance?
- Any restrictions in the condominium or HOA?
- Do they allow pets and what size?
- Can I put a lockbox or electronic lockbox on the house? (for a vacant house)
- What do you think an agent should do to sell your house at a higher price?
- Do you want me to handle the sale for you?

Why work with me?

- I am a full-time real estate agent
- I will do open houses and/or virtual open houses
- I will promote your listing in all social media, email, mail, and websites
- I will invest 100% of my effort, time, and money into selling your property
- If you are not happy with my service, you can fire me
- I love real estate and I love representing the seller side
- My team and I have #____ years of experience
- I will do my best to sell your property for the highest price at the fastest time
- I promise to keep you up-to-date on the progress of your sale at least once a week by phone or email and will share buyer feedback about your home after each showing.

The Importance of Pricing & Why You Should Price Realistically

- If a property is priced right, it will sell faster and with the best buyers possible in the area.
- The property will be exposed to all ready, willing, and able buyers.
- Most of the time you will get multiple offers. It will be easier to sell even for a higher price than the list price
- The price is rarely reduced.
- The appraisal will come in at the correct value.
- When the property is overpriced, not all buyers will see the property, and you will lose real buyers.
- More time in the market tends to receive lower offers.
- Most offers come in at less than the asking price.
- Buyers educate themselves and know what a fair price is.
- Overpricing causes most properties to remain on the market for a long time and buyers are afraid to make offers thinking that "something is wrong with the house." Some overpriced homes tend to sell for even less.
- If a seller already bought another house, they could end up paying two mortgages at the same time.

Property History

Median Estimated Home Value

This chart displays property estimates for an area and a subject property, where one has been selected. Estimated home values are generated by a valuation model and are not formal appraisals.

Data Source: Valuation calculations based on public records and MLS sources where licensed

Update Frequency: Monthly

- This House
- 33141
- Miami-Dade County
- Florida

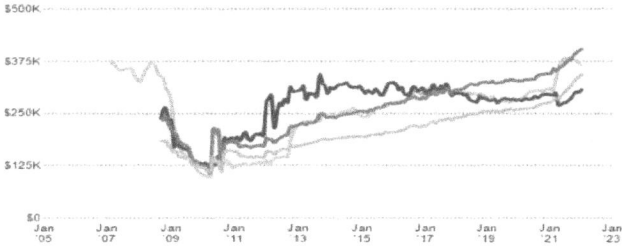

Sales History

Sales Date	Sales Amount	Price per sq. ft.
7/29/2016	$313,000	$295
10/17/2012	$250,000	$235
4/5/2012	$139,300	$131
9/12/2006	$335,000	$315
8/6/2003	$252,900	$238

Assessed Values

Date	Improvements	Land	Total	Tax
2021	--	--	$238,700	$5,369
2020	--	--	$220,979	$4,948
2019	--	--	$266,240	$5,829
2018	--	--	$256,000	$5,829
2017	--	--	$242,949	$5,309
2016	--	--	$231,380	--
2015	--	--	$201,200	$4,535
2014	--	--	$179,640	$4,142
2013	--	--	$166,330	$3,858
2012	--	--	$106,620	$2,409
2011	--	--	$101,540	$2,307
2010	--	--	$126,920	--
2009	--	--	$192,300	--
2008	--	--	$349,630	--
2007	--	--	$513,930	--

Legal Description

APN:	Tax ID:	Zoning:	Census Tract:	Abbreviated Description:	City/Municipality/Township:
23-3209-041-4230	--	6300:COMMERCIAL_RESTRICT	120860039.171001	CITY/MUNI/TWP:NORTH BAY VILLAGE SEC/TWN/RNG/MER:SEC 09 TWN 53S RNG 42E THE GRANDVIEW PALACE CONDO UNIT 818 UNDIV 0.19587% INT IN COMMON ELEMENTS OFF REC 21423-3980 COC 24900-2663 08 2006 1	North Bay Village, FL 33141

---

123 Main Street, Miami, Fl. 33165

Legend: ⊙ Subject Property

● Active   · Active: 3/12/2021

List Price
$425,000
Active Date: 3/12/2021
Listing ID: A11013079

Current Estimated Value
$363,810
Last RVM® Update: 1/25/2022
RVM® Est. Range: $324K – $404K
RVM® Confidence: ★★★★☆
↑ RVM® Change - Last 1 Month: $4,490
↑ RVM® Change - Last 12 Months: 15.73%

Your Comp Analysis
$401,412
Last Edited: 2/14/2022
$378 Price per Sq. Ft.
Your Comp Analysis Range
$351K – $475K

Price per Bedroom of Homes Sold

This chart shows the distribution of homes reported sold in the past six months at different prices per bedroom in the area of your search. The amount shown for the subject property is sold data where available, or the property's estimated value when sales data are unavailable (such as a non-disclosure state) or provided in range format.

Data Source: Public records and MLS data where licensed

Update Frequency: Monthly

▨ This House
■ Comps

This House
$182K   1

Comps
$225K - $250K   2
$175K - $200K   10
$150K - $175K   4

Median Sales Price by Square Footage

This chart shows the median price of homes reported sold in the past six months, according to the size of the living space (square footage sourced from public records). The amount shown for the subject property is sold data where available, or the property's estimated value when sales data are unavailable (such as non-disclosure states) or provided in range format.

Data Source: Public records and MLS data where licensed

Update Frequency: Monthly

▨ This House
■ Comps

This House
1,061 sq. ft. $363,810

Comps
1,000 - 1,200 sq. ft. $374,750

HOW THIS ZIP COMPARES:

Miami Beach, FL 33141

More About this Neighborhood

Median Estimated Home Value   About this data

33141	$302,940
Miami-Dade	$404,890
Florida	$344,180

12 mo. Change in Median Estimated Home Value   About this data

33141	4.2%
Miami-Dade	16.7%
Florida	23.9%

Median Listing Sales Price   About this data

33141	$385,000
Miami-Dade	$436,500
Florida	$345,000

Median Public Sales Price   About this data

33141	$317,000
Miami-Dade	$410,000
Florida	$332,000

Median Listing Price   About this data

33141	$439,000
Miami-Dade	$460,000
Florida	$364,900

12 mo. Change in Median Listing Price   About this data

33141	10.0%
Miami-Dade	10.3%
Florida	21.1%

Median Days in RPR   About this data

33141	98
Miami-Dade	86
Florida	58

12 mo. Change in Median Days in RPR   About this data

33141	-11.0%
Miami-Dade	-2%.2%
Florida	-22.7%

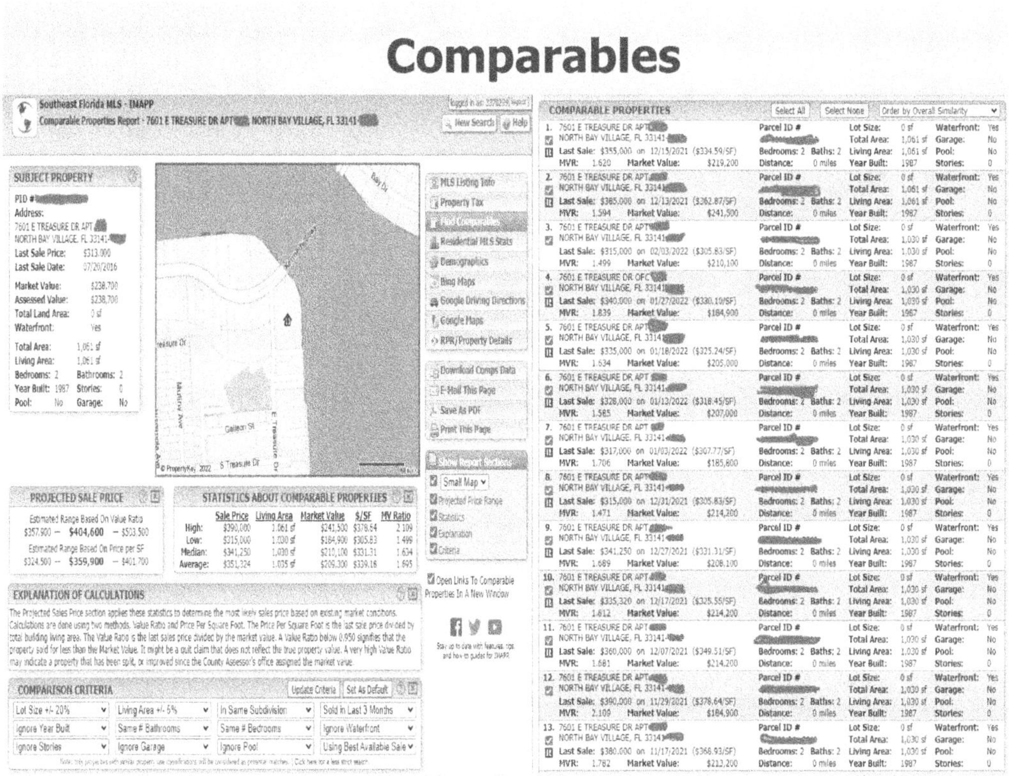
Comparables
Southeast Florida MLS - IMAPP
SUBJECT PROPERTY
PROJECTED SALE PRICE
STATISTICS ABOUT COMPARABLE PROPERTIES
EXPLANATION OF CALCULATIONS
COMPARISON CRITERIA
COMPARABLE PROPERTIES

Comps and Adjustments
This Property
Active
7601 E Treasure Dr, Apt [redacted]
North Bay Village, FL 33141
[redacted] days
$401 1,061 sqft 2 2 1987
Listings
Pending
7601 E Treasure Dr, Ph [redacted]
North Bay Village, FL 33141
– Mi. E 20 days 1/25/2022 $469,000 $442 1,061 sqft 2 2 1987 Same
Active
7601 E Treasure Dr, Apt [redacted]
North Bay Village, FL 33141
– Mi. E 43 days 1/2/2022 $475,000 $448 1,061 sqft 2 2 1987 Same
Active
7601 E Treasure Dr, Apt [redacted]
North Bay Village, FL 33141
– Mi. E 52 days 12/24/2021 $375,000 $353 1,061 sqft 2 2 1987 Same
Recently Sold
RPR
2/15/2022
MIAMI REALTORS
Property Report
7601 E Treasure Dr, Apt 818, [redacted] Bay Village, FL 33141
Closed
7601 E Treasure Dr, Apt [redacted]
North Bay Village, FL 33141
– Mi. E – 12/6/2021 $358,000 $333 1,074 sqft 2 2 1987 Same
Closed
7601 E Treasure Dr, Apt [redacted]
North Bay Village, FL 33141
– Mi. E 9 days 12/3/2021 $385,000 $363 1,061 sqft 2 2 1987 Same
Closed
7601 E Treasure Dr, Apt [redacted]
North Bay Village, FL 33141
– Mi. E – 12/13/2021 $355,000 $331 1,074 sqft 2 2 1987 Same

Comparables

Comparable Market Analysis

Recommended Pricing Strategy

This chart compares the high, low and median price of homes in various listing statuses in the subject property's ZIP code to help determine the asking price for the subject property. The prices of the User Selected Comps are closed prices where available.

	User Selected Comps	Market Activity For Sale Listings	Market Activity Closed	Market Activity Distressed	Market Activity Expired Listings	Market Activity Pending Sales
Lowest Price	$355,000	$205,000	$128,000	$142,820	$160,000	$185,000
Median Price	$380,000	$422,500	$176,750	$203,810	$427,500	$409,000
Highest Price	$475,000	$1,530,000	$1,025,000	$490,900	$3,995,000	$1,250,000
Median Price Per Sq. Ft.	$358	$421	$333	$265	$367	$447
Median Days in RPR	32	1	96	39	181	20

Sold Price Comparison

This section compares prices for 76 properties in the subject property's ZIP code with a similar number of beds and baths, sold within the past 90 days.

	Sold Price	Price Per Sq. Ft.
Lowest Price	$195,000	$175
Median Price	$382,500	$327
Highest Price	$1,850,000	$1,286

Details of Comparative Analysis

Average of Comps	$401,412
Adjustments	—
Adjusted Value	$401,412 (or $378 per sq. ft.)

Easy Exit, Love it or Leave it!

I understand that the biggest fear a seller has is being locked into a long-term listing agreement. For this reason, I offer an easy exit listing agreement.

Yes, you can fire me if you do not love the job I'm doing or how I am representing you.

You can cancel your listing anytime and relax knowing you are not locked into a contract you do not want to continue.

I am confident enough to make this offer to you because I know you will love my service.

**If you list your property with me today,
I will give you a $500.00 bonus
toward your closing costs**

Thank you!

**Thanks for the opportunity to sell your property
with me!**

The End

Showing a Property Virtually for a Buyer or Tenant

Since the start of the pandemic, more agents have been showing properties virtually. In the past it had been used to work with clients in other states and countries. You can show properties in many ways such as:

- Take a video of each property you see and send it to your clients. Many agents have done this in the past, and it's still effective.
- Create a link first and invite your client to it or invite your client from the Zoom meeting as soon as you get into the first property on your cell phone. Start the video and record the meeting with your client. When you use Zoom, it is easy to interact with your client. At the same time, you can record everything and send each video separately. You can ask questions as if you have the client there with you in the showing and use your sales techniques. You will easily know which house they prefer on the day of the showing, so when you finish, you can send the purchase contract immediately or the contract to lease if they are a tenant. Another benefit is that you can invite all the people involved in the transaction and record to the Zoom cloud (if you pay for the Pro subscription). This keeps you from using up your cell phone storage and is easier to send via the Zoom link.
- Google Meet, Vimeo, and other platforms allow you to Facetime, record the meeting, and invite several participants.

Always use your sales techniques as if you have your client in front of you.

Virtual Open House

Having a virtual open house at the same time you have your in-person open house is an excellent way to approach more clients and sell the property faster. Another benefit is the great potential to have the open house event live on social media. You look great to your client, and you get more buyers, sellers, tenants, and landlords. Virtual-only is a great way to do an open house when sellers do not want people on their property.

To advertise the virtual open house, use Zoom or Google Meet to record yourself and share the link. You could also use any social media's live option or upload a recording to Vimeo and put the link on all social media. Advertise the link and invite as many participants as possible. The in-person open house could be for two hours, and the live event could be for 30 minutes to show the property and answer any questions that people might have.

The best way to do the virtual open house is via your cell phone so you can move around the property or put it on a small table to show the in-person open house.

Buy equipment for your cell phone or tablet to help you do the live event easier, such as a tripod for added functionality.

If you do a double event such as an in-person open house and a virtual open house, bring a person to help you when you are having the virtual event. You'll want to be able to talk with virtual attendees and show them the property. If someone comes to the open house, the other person can help you with them in person or take over the virtual open house.

Always advertise and promote the open house event on the MLS as two different events; for the in-person event, say "public" in the open house type and for the virtual, say "virtual public." Remember to first create the link so you can add it to the Live Stream/Recorded Open House URL. In addition, advertise with the link on all your social media and with neighbors, coworkers, agents, and potential clients.

The day of the event, always get the contact information for all the people who attend.

Postcard samples for the open house:

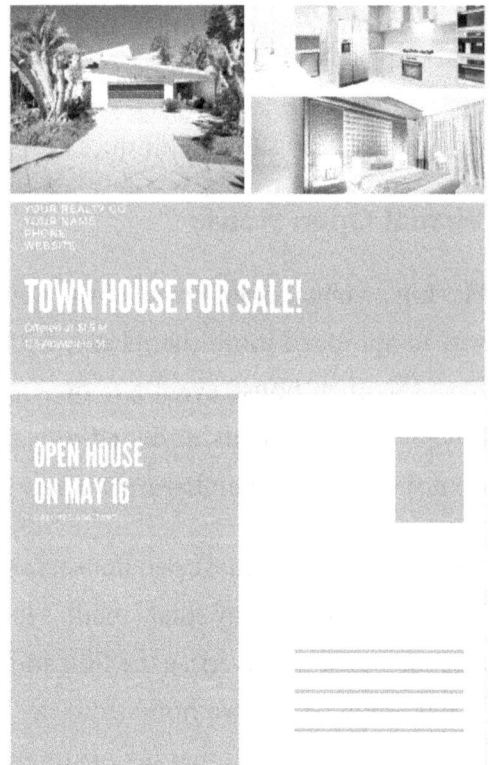

Chapter 6

Residential Contracts

We will work through the first one or two pages of some of the contracts we have talked about in this book: residential contract for sale and purchase between the buyer and seller, listing agreements either for sale or for rent, the CTL contract-to-lease, and the lease agreement. For a deeper study and explanation of additional real estate contracts, you can obtain *The Fearless Agent Series Book 3 For Contracts*. This book is a detailed study for each type of real estate contract, blank and filled out, including their respective addendums. It includes contracts for vacant land, commercial business opportunities, and more.

Before you prepare a contract, make sure you have at least:

- The MLS listing of the property printed out or on your computer.
- IMAPP printed or on your computer.
- The letter of prequalification to fill out the correct financing information or proof of funds if it is a cash offer.
- The Form Simplicity program, the program your board uses, or the contracts and respective addendums you will need to write the offer (always have an extra copy if you are going to prepare it on paper).
- Escrow agent information.

"AS IS" Residential Contract for Sale and Purchase

These first 2 pages are the most important in a residential for sale and purchase contract. The example is an "as is" contract. It does not matter if it is an as is contract or not. The most important thing is to fill out everything that is required. I will use the numbers inside the parenthesis to explain the most important things in the contract.

"AS IS" Residential Contract For Sale And Purchase

THIS FORM HAS BEEN APPROVED BY THE FLORIDA REALTORS AND THE FLORIDA BAR

FloridaRealtors®

1* **PARTIES:** _____ ("Seller"),
2* and _____ ("Buyer"),
3 agree that Seller shall sell and Buyer shall buy the following described Real Property and Personal Property
4 (collectively "Property") pursuant to the terms and conditions of this AS IS Residential Contract For Sale And Purchase
5 and any riders and addenda ("Contract"):

6 **1. PROPERTY DESCRIPTION:**
7*   (a) Street address, city, zip: _____
8*   (b) Located in: _____ County, Florida. Property Tax ID #: _____
9*   (c) Real Property: The legal description is _____
10   _____
11   _____
12   together with all existing improvements and fixtures, including built-in appliances, built-in furnishings and
13   attached wall-to-wall carpeting and flooring ("Real Property") unless specifically excluded in Paragraph 1(e) or
14   by other terms of this Contract.
15   (d) Personal Property: Unless excluded in Paragraph 1(e) or by other terms of this Contract, the following items
16   which are owned by Seller and existing on the Property as of the date of the initial offer are included in the
17   purchase: range(s)/oven(s), refrigerator(s), dishwasher(s), disposal, ceiling fan(s), light fixture(s), drapery rods
18   and draperies, blinds, window treatments, smoke detector(s), garage door opener(s), thermostat(s),
19   doorbell(s), television wall mount(s) and television mounting hardware, security gate and other access
20   devices, mailbox keys, and storm shutters/storm protection items and hardware ("Personal Property").
21*   Other Personal Property items included in this purchase are: _____
22   _____
23   Personal Property is included in the Purchase Price, has no contributory value, and shall be left for the Buyer.
24*   (e) The following items are excluded from the purchase: _____
25   _____

26* **PURCHASE PRICE AND CLOSING**

27* **2. PURCHASE PRICE** (U.S. currency):...$ _____
28*   (a) Initial deposit to be held in escrow in the amount of (**checks subject to Collection**) ...... $ _____
29   The initial deposit made payable and delivered to "Escrow Agent" named below
30*   (**CHECK ONE**): (i) ☐ accompanies offer or (ii) ☐ is to be made within _____ (if left
31   blank, then 3) days after Effective Date. IF NEITHER BOX IS CHECKED, THEN
32   OPTION (ii) SHALL BE DEEMED SELECTED.
33*   Escrow Agent Name: _____
34*   Address: _____ Phone: _____
35*   E-mail: _____ Fax: _____
36*   (b) Additional deposit to be delivered to Escrow Agent within _____ (if left blank, then 10)
37*   days after Effective Date ....$ _____
38   (All deposits paid or agreed to be paid, are collectively referred to as the "Deposit")
39*   (c) Financing: Express as a dollar amount or percentage ("Loan Amount") see Paragraph 8 .... _____
40*   (d) Other: _____ .... $ _____
41   (e) Balance to close (not including Buyer's closing costs, prepaids and prorations) by wire
42*   transfer or other Collected funds (see STANDARD S)...............$ _____

43 **3. TIME FOR ACCEPTANCE OF OFFER AND COUNTER-OFFERS; EFFECTIVE DATE:**
44   (a) If not signed by Buyer and Seller, and an executed copy delivered to all parties on or before
45*   _____, this offer shall be deemed withdrawn and the Deposit, if any, shall be returned to
46   Buyer. Unless otherwise stated, time for acceptance of any counter-offers shall be within 2 days after the day
47   the counter-offer is delivered.
48   (b) The effective date of this Contract shall be the date when the last one of the Buyer and Seller has signed or
49   initialed and delivered this offer or final counter-offer ("Effective Date").

50 **4. CLOSING; CLOSING DATE:** The closing of this transaction shall occur when all funds required for closing are
51 received by Closing Agent and Collected pursuant to STANDARD S and all closing documents required to be
52 furnished by each party pursuant to this Contract are delivered ("Closing"). Unless modified by other provisions of

53* this Contract, the Closing shall occur on _____ ("Closing Date"), at the time
54 established by the Closing Agent.

5. EXTENSION OF CLOSING DATE:

55 (a) In the event Closing funds from Buyer's lender(s) are not available on Closing Date due to Consumer Financial
56 Protection Bureau Closing Disclosure delivery requirements ("CFPB Requirements"), if Paragraph 8(b) is
57 checked, Loan Approval has been obtained, and lender's underwriting is complete, then Closing Date shall be
58 extended for such period necessary to satisfy CFPB Requirements, provided such period shall not exceed 7
59 days.
60
61 (b) If an event constituting "Force Majeure" causes services essential for Closing to be unavailable, including the
62 unavailability of utilities or issuance of hazard, wind, flood or homeowners' insurance, Closing Date shall be
63 extended as provided in STANDARD G.

6. OCCUPANCY AND POSSESSION:

65 (a) Unless Paragraph 6(b) is checked, Seller shall, at Closing, deliver occupancy and possession of the Property
66 to Buyer free of tenants, occupants and future tenancies. Also, at Closing, Seller shall have removed all
67 personal items and trash from the Property and shall deliver all keys, garage door openers, access devices and
68* codes, as applicable, to Buyer. If occupancy is to be delivered before Closing, Buyer assumes all risks of loss
69 to the Property from date of occupancy, shall be responsible and liable for maintenance from that date, and
70 shall have accepted the Property in its existing condition as of time of taking occupancy, see Rider T PRE-
71 CLOSING OCCUPANCY BY BUYER.

72* (b) ☐ **CHECK IF PROPERTY IS SUBJECT TO LEASE(S) OR OCCUPANCY AFTER CLOSING.** If Property is
73 subject to a lease(s) or any occupancy agreements (including seasonal and short-term vacation rentals) after
74 Closing or is intended to be rented or occupied by third parties beyond Closing, the facts and terms thereof
75 shall be disclosed in writing by Seller to Buyer and copies of the written lease(s) shall be delivered to Buyer, all
76 within 5 days after Effective Date. If Buyer determines, in Buyer's sole discretion, that the lease(s) or terms of
77* occupancy are not acceptable to Buyer, Buyer may terminate this Contract by delivery of written notice of such
78* election to Seller within 5 days after receipt of the above items from Seller, and Buyer shall be refunded the
79 Deposit thereby releasing Buyer and Seller from all further obligations under this Contract. Estoppel Letter(s)
80 and Seller's affidavit shall be provided pursuant to STANDARD D, except that tenant Estoppel Letters shall not
81 be required on seasonal or short-term vacation rentals. If Property is intended to be occupied by Seller after
82 Closing, see Rider U POST-CLOSING OCCUPANCY BY SELLER.

83* **7. ASSIGNABILITY: (CHECK ONE):** Buyer ☐ may assign and thereby be released from any further liability under
84* this Contract; ☐ may assign but not be released from liability under this Contract; or ☐ may not assign this Contract.
85 IF NO BOX IS CHECKED, THEN BUYER MAY NOT ASSIGN THIS CONTRACT.

86 **FINANCING**

8. FINANCING:

88* ☐ (a) This is a cash transaction with no financing contingency.

89* ☐ (b) This Contract is contingent upon, within _____ (if left blank, then 30) days after Effective Date ("Loan
90* Approval Period"): (1) Buyer obtaining approval of a ☐conventional ☐FHA ☐VA or ☐other _____
91* (describe) mortgage loan for purchase of the Property for a **(CHECK ONE):** ☐fixed, ☐adjustable, ☐fixed or
92 adjustable rate in the Loan Amount (See Paragraph 2(c)), at an initial interest rate not to exceed _____ % (if left
93 blank, then prevailing rate based upon Buyer's creditworthiness), and for a term of _____ (if left blank, then 30)
94 years ("Financing"); and (2) Buyer's mortgage broker or lender having received an appraisal or alternative valuation
95 of the Property satisfactory to lender, if either is required by lender, which is sufficient to meet the terms required
96 for lender to provide Financing for Buyer and proceed to Closing ("Appraisal").

97* (i) Buyer shall make application for Financing within _____ (if left blank, then 5) days after Effective Date
98 and use good faith and diligent effort to obtain approval of a loan meeting the Financing and Appraisal terms of
99 Paragraph 8(b)(1) and (2), above, ("Loan Approval") within the Loan Approval Period and, thereafter, to close this
100 Contract. Loan Approval which requires Buyer to sell other real property shall not be considered Loan Approval
101 unless Rider V is attached.
102 Buyer's failure to use good faith and diligent effort to obtain Loan Approval during the Loan Approval Period shall
103 be considered a default under the terms of this Contract. For purposes of this provision, "diligent effort" includes,
104 but is not limited to, timely furnishing all documents and information required by Buyer's mortgage broker and lender
105 and paying for Appraisal and other fees and charges in connection with Buyer's application for Financing.
106 (ii) Buyer shall, upon written request, keep Seller and Broker fully informed about the status of Buyer's
107 mortgage loan application, loan processing, appraisal, and Loan Approval, including any Property related conditions
108 of Loan Approval. Buyer authorizes Buyer's mortgage broker, lender, and Closing Agent to disclose such status

Gather all the information for the parties involved, then go to IMAPP and MLS to get most of the property and seller information:

(1) Name of seller(s) which could be a company. The information is in IMAPP (county tax data/ report), and other platforms.

(2) Buyer(s) name or company name

(6) 1. Property Description

(7) (a) Property address. When you are in the MLS, just click on the folio number and it will take you to IMAPP. Copy and paste the address.

(8) (b) County and property tax ID#, (found it in the MLS, IMAPP, etc.)

(9-11) (c) The legal description, on IMAPP, MLS, etc.

(15) (d) Explanation of what is considered personal property

(21-22) Other Personal Property items included in this purchase; the same as it is in the MLS under additional information, in equipment/appliances

(24-25) (e) Items excluded from the purchase, such as a chandelier

(27) 2. Purchase price $ _____

(28) (a) Initial deposit $ _____

(30-32) Check one of the ☐ boxes to let the seller know how the deposit is going to be made. Example: (i) ☐ accompanies offer, or (ii) ☐ is to be made within _____ (# of days after executed) _____ (the deposit is not with the offer, if left blank, then it will be three days. If neither box is checked, then option (ii) shall be deemed selected.

(33) Name of the escrow agent. Example: Title company, Attorney, Real Estate company

(34) Escrow agent address and phone number

(35) Escrow agent email and fax

(36) (b) Additional deposit (only if your client will do an additional deposit, put 0 or n/a if there will be no additional deposit), within _____ (# of days). If you leave the space of # of days in blank, it will be within ten days.

(37-38) Amount of the second deposit $ _____

(39) (c) Financing: Expressed as a dollar amount or percentage. Example: $80,000 (if it is a sale price of $100,000 and financed at 80%) or just put the percentage. Example: 80%. I prefer to put a percentage since the system does the calculation in case you put the wrong amount. If the sales price changes, the percentage will be the same.

(40) (d) Other: This means other loans, such as an owner finance or a second mortgage.

(41-42) Balance to close (not including other costs related to the purchase such as closing costs, prepaid expenses, and prorations) $ _____

(43)3. Time for Acceptance of Offer and Counteroffer; Effective Date

(44-47) (a) If not signed on or before _____ by this date and an executed copy delivered by all parties, this offer will be withdrawn unless otherwise stated. Usually, it is good to put 2-3 business days to be fair and safe.

(48)(b) Explanation of what the term of "Effective date" means, which is the last signature and/or initial of the buyer and/or seller and delivery to all parties.

(50)4. Closing, Closing Date

(53) The closing should occur on _____ or before _____ (closing date). It is important to use a realistic date, so you do not end up out of contract especially with finance companies. You can put a date or the phrase "on or before" the date you know you expect to close. This means that you can close before or on the agreed date.

(55) 5. Extension of closing date

(56-60) (a) An additional extension up to 7 days only for buyers who are using financing and if the financing requires an additional extension. Only if Buyer checks paragraph 8 (b)

(61-63) (b) Only for "force majeure" cause. The closing should be extended due to hurricane, flood, etc. Explanation on STANDARD G.

(64-82) 6. Occupancy and possession

(65-71) (a) Seller shall deliver the property without any tenant, free of any occupancy. If the buyer occupies the property before closing, the buyer is responsible for everything from the time they occupy the property.

(72-82) (b) When the buyer closes, but if the seller continues to live in or is a tenant in the property. The buyer can cancel the contract if after he/she reviews all contracts the buyer is not comfortable with the contract he/she can cancel.

(83-85) 7. Assignability. The buyer can choose that the contract can be assigned or not assigned. If no box is checked, the contract is not assignable.

(87) 8. Finance

(88) (a) Cash purchase with no finance contingency

(89-92) (b) Finance contingency. Term of loan including type of loan, interest, and more. The buyer should inform the seller of the process of the loan.

"AS IS" Residential Contract For Sale And Purchase
THIS FORM HAS BEEN APPROVED BY THE FLORIDA REALTORS AND THE FLORIDA BAR

FloridaRealtors®

1* PARTIES: _____ John Doe _____ ("Seller"),
2* and _____ Mary Smith _____ ("Buyer"),
3   agree that Seller shall sell and Buyer shall buy the following described Real Property and Personal Property
4   (collectively "Property") pursuant to the terms and conditions of this AS IS Residential Contract For Sale And Purchase
5   and any riders and addenda ("Contract"):
6   **1. PROPERTY DESCRIPTION:**
7*   (a) Street address, city, zip: _____ 123 Main Street, Miami, Florida 33111 _____
8*   (b) Located in: ___Miami___ County, Florida. Property Tax ID #: _____ 1234567890123 _____
9*   (c) Real Property: The legal description is and#xA4;GRAND CANAL SUB PB 100-00 Lot 1 BLK 1 LOT SIZE
10   70.000 X 100 OR 12345-678 9101 2
11
12   together with all existing improvements and fixtures, including built-in appliances, built-in furnishings and
13   attached wall-to-wall carpeting and flooring ("Real Property") unless specifically excluded in Paragraph 1(e) or
14   by other terms of this Contract.
15   (d) Personal Property: Unless excluded in Paragraph 1(e) or by other terms of this Contract, the following items
16   which are owned by Seller and existing on the Property as of the date of the initial offer are included in the
17   purchase: range(s)/oven(s), refrigerator(s), dishwasher(s), disposal, ceiling fan(s), light fixture(s), drapery rods
18   and draperies, blinds, window treatments, smoke detector(s), garage door opener(s), thermostat(s),
19   doorbell(s), television wall mount(s) and television mounting hardware, security gate and other access
20   devices, mailbox keys, and storm shutters/storm protection items and hardware ("Personal Property").
21*   Other Personal Property items included in this purchase are: Washer, dryer, stove, refrigerator, microwave,
22   fan
23   Personal Property is included in the Purchase Price, has no contributory value, and shall be left for the Buyer.
24*   (e) The following items are excluded from the purchase: Chandelier
25

PURCHASE PRICE AND CLOSING

27* **2. PURCHASE PRICE** (U.S. currency):.. $ 500,000.00
28*   (a) Initial deposit to be held in escrow in the amount of **(checks subject to Collection)** ...... $ 5,000.00
29   The initial deposit made payable and delivered to "Escrow Agent" named below
30*   **(CHECK ONE):** (i) [X] accompanies offer or (ii) [ ] is to be made within _____ (if left
31   blank, then 3) days after Effective Date. IF NEITHER BOX IS CHECKED, THEN
32   OPTION (ii) SHALL BE DEEMED SELECTED.
33*   Escrow Agent Name: _____ Any Title Company _____
34*   Address: ___111 SW 22 Street, Any city, Florida 33111___ Phone: 305-123-4567
35*   E-mail: ___anytitle@gmail.com___ Fax: 305-123-4568
36*   (b) Additional deposit to be delivered to Escrow Agent within ___5___ (if left blank, then 10)
37*   days after Effective Date .... $ 5,000.00
38   (All deposits paid or agreed to be paid, are collectively referred to as the "Deposit")
39*   (c) Financing: Express as a dollar amount or percentage ("Loan Amount") see Paragraph 8 .... 80%
40*   (d) Other: _____ N/A _____ $ 0.00
41   (e) Balance to close (not including Buyer's closing costs, prepaids and prorations) by wire
42*   transfer or other Collected funds (see STANDARD S)........................... $ 90,000.00
43   **3. TIME FOR ACCEPTANCE OF OFFER AND COUNTER-OFFERS; EFFECTIVE DATE:**
44   (a) If not signed by Buyer and Seller, and an executed copy delivered to all parties on or before
45*   ____March 1, 2022____, this offer shall be deemed withdrawn and the Deposit, if any, shall be returned to
46   Buyer. Unless otherwise stated, time for acceptance of any counter-offers shall be within 2 days after the day
47   the counter-offer is delivered.
48   (b) The effective date of this Contract shall be the date when the last one of the Buyer and Seller has signed or
49   initialed and delivered this offer or final counter-offer ("Effective Date").
50   **4. CLOSING; CLOSING DATE:** The closing of this transaction shall occur when all funds required for closing are
51   received by Closing Agent and Collected pursuant to STANDARD S and all closing documents required to be
52   furnished by each party pursuant to this Contract are delivered ("Closing"). Unless modified by other provisions of

this Contract, the Closing shall occur on _____On or before April 30, 2022_____ ("Closing Date"), at the time established by the Closing Agent.

5. EXTENSION OF CLOSING DATE:

(a) In the event Closing funds from Buyer's lender(s) are not available on Closing Date due to Consumer Financial Protection Bureau Closing Disclosure delivery requirements ("CFPB Requirements"), if Paragraph 8(b) is checked, Loan Approval has been obtained, and lender's underwriting is complete, then Closing Date shall be extended for such period necessary to satisfy CFPB Requirements, provided such period shall not exceed 7 days.

(b) If an event constituting "Force Majeure" causes services essential for Closing to be unavailable, including the unavailability of utilities or issuance of hazard, wind, flood or homeowners' insurance, Closing Date shall be extended as provided in STANDARD G.

6. OCCUPANCY AND POSSESSION:

(a) Unless Paragraph 6(b) is checked, Seller shall, at Closing, deliver occupancy and possession of the Property to Buyer free of tenants, occupants and future tenancies. Also, at Closing, Seller shall have removed all personal items and trash from the Property and shall deliver all keys, garage door openers, access devices and codes, as applicable, to Buyer. If occupancy is to be delivered before Closing, Buyer assumes all risks of loss to the Property from date of occupancy, shall be responsible and liable for maintenance from that date, and shall have accepted the Property in its existing condition as of time of taking occupancy, see Rider T PRE-CLOSING OCCUPANCY BY BUYER.

(b) ☐ **CHECK IF PROPERTY IS SUBJECT TO LEASE(S) OR OCCUPANCY AFTER CLOSING.** If Property is subject to a lease(s) or any occupancy agreements (including seasonal and short-term vacation rentals) after Closing or is intended to be rented or occupied by third parties beyond Closing, the facts and terms thereof shall be disclosed in writing by Seller to Buyer and copies of the written lease(s) shall be delivered to Buyer, all within 5 days after Effective Date. If Buyer determines, in Buyer's sole discretion, that the lease(s) or terms of occupancy are not acceptable to Buyer, Buyer may terminate this Contract by delivery of written notice of such election to Seller within 5 days after receipt of the above items from Seller, and Buyer shall be refunded the Deposit thereby releasing Buyer and Seller from all further obligations under this Contract. Estoppel Letter(s) and Seller's affidavit shall be provided pursuant to STANDARD D, except that tenant Estoppel Letters shall not be required on seasonal or short-term vacation rentals. If Property is intended to be occupied by Seller after Closing, see Rider U POST-CLOSING OCCUPANCY BY SELLER.

7. ASSIGNABILITY: (CHECK ONE): Buyer ☐ may assign and thereby be released from any further liability under this Contract; ☐ may assign but not be released from liability under this Contract; or ☐ may not assign this Contract. IF NO BOX IS CHECKED, THEN BUYER MAY NOT ASSIGN THIS CONTRACT.

FINANCING

8. FINANCING:

☐ (a) This is a cash transaction with no financing contingency.

☒ (b) This Contract is contingent upon, within _____ (if left blank, then 30) days after Effective Date ("Loan Approval Period"). (1) Buyer obtaining approval of a ☒ conventional ☐ FHA ☐ VA or ☐ other _____ (describe) mortgage loan for purchase of the Property for a **(CHECK ONE):** ☒ fixed, ☐ adjustable, ☐ fixed or adjustable rate in the Loan Amount (See Paragraph 2(c)), at an initial interest rate not to exceed _____ % (if left blank, then prevailing rate based upon Buyer's creditworthiness), and for a term of _____ (if left blank, then 30) years ("Financing"); and (2) Buyer's mortgage broker or lender having received an appraisal or alternative valuation of the Property satisfactory to lender, if either is required by lender, which is sufficient to meet the terms required for lender to provide Financing for Buyer and proceed to Closing ("Appraisal").

(i) Buyer shall make application for Financing within _____ (if left blank, then 5) days after Effective Date and use good faith and diligent effort to obtain approval of a loan meeting the Financing and Appraisal terms of Paragraph 8(b)(1) and (2), above, ("Loan Approval") within the Loan Approval Period and, thereafter, to close this Contract. Loan Approval which requires Buyer to sell other real property shall not be considered Loan Approval unless Rider V is attached.

Buyer's failure to use good faith and diligent effort to obtain Loan Approval during the Loan Approval Period shall be considered a default under the terms of this Contract. For purposes of this provision, "diligent effort" includes, but is not limited to, timely furnishing all documents and information required by Buyer's mortgage broker and lender and paying for Appraisal and other fees and charges in connection with Buyer's application for Financing.

(ii) Buyer shall, upon written request, keep Seller and Broker fully informed about the status of Buyer's mortgage loan application, loan processing, appraisal, and Loan Approval, including any Property related conditions of Loan Approval. Buyer authorizes Buyer's mortgage broker, lender, and Closing Agent to disclose such status

Buyer's Initials _____   Page **2** of **12**   Seller's Initials _____ _____

Serial#: 022237-400164-5136091

Form Simplicity

Exclusive Right of Sale Listing Agreement

This agreement is between the agent/broker and the owner of the property. Both must date, sign, and initial the contract. This agreement has an initial and a termination date. We will discuss just the first page of this agreement.

You can prefill it or write it with the seller. When the seller lives in another state or is far from the property, you can have a virtual presentation and send the agreement by email. Some agents use Form Simplicity or other programs to prefill their name, company name, and commission to make it easier to create new listing agreements.

(2) Seller name. Get his/her name from the MLS.

(3) Real estate company name or broker name.

(4) 1. The first paragraph says that the extension of the date is automatically extended through the actual closing date if this contract becomes a contract for sale.

(6) Beginning date _____, termination date _____ of the listing agreement.

(12) 2. Information about the property that you can get from the seller and from IMAPP or any tax data program.

(13) (a) Property address: _____

(15-16) Legal Description: Find it on IMAPP or the county's tax data and mark ☐ see attachment if any.

(17-18) (b) Personal property that will be included in the sale _____,
☐ see attachment if any

(19-20) (c) Occupancy: check if is ☐ vacant or ☐ occupied by a tenant and when the lease expires.

(21) 3. Price and terms that the seller tells you to use after advising them with a CMA (comparable market analysis).

(22) (a) Price $ _____

(23) (b) Financing Terms: select all that apply. If it is a condo, do not ☐ check FHA or VA if you are not sure if the condo association accepts this type of financing.

(24-36) Seller Financing: check this only if the seller will finance the purchase, has a purchase money mortgage, or an assumable mortgage. If they do, ask for all the conditions of this mortgage.

(37-38) (c) Seller expenses that they agree to pay _____%. This paragraph is important to approach because some buyers will need help with closing costs. Some sellers may be willing to cooperate with some buyer closing costs.

Exclusive Right of Sale Listing Agreement

FloridaRealtors

1 This Exclusive Right of Sale Listing Agreement ("Agreement") is between

2" _____ ("**Seller**")

3" and _____ ("**Broker**").

4   1. **Authority to Sell Property:** **Seller** gives **Broker** the EXCLUSIVE RIGHT TO SELL the real and personal
5   property (collectively "Property") described below, at the price and terms described below, beginning
6"   _____ and terminating at 11:59 p.m. on _____ ("Termination Date"). Upon
7   full execution of a contract for sale and purchase of the Property, all rights and obligations of this Agreement will
8   automatically extend through the date of the actual closing of the sales contract. **Seller** and **Broker** acknowledge
9   that this Agreement does not guarantee a sale. This Property will be offered to any person without regard to race,
10   color, religion, sex, handicap, familial status, national origin, or any other factor protected by federal, state, or local
11   law. **Seller** certifies and represents that she/he/it is legally entitled to convey the Property and all improvements.

12 2. **Description of Property:**
13"   (a) **Street Address:** _____

14   _____

15"   Legal Description: _____

16"   _____ ☐ See Attachment _____

17"   (b) **Personal Property, including appliances:** _____

18"   _____ ☐ See Attachment _____

19   (c) **Occupancy:**
20"   Property ☐ is ☐ is not currently occupied by a tenant. If occupied, the lease term expires _____.

21 3. **Price and Terms:** The property is offered for sale on the following terms or on other terms acceptable to **Seller**:
22"   (a) **Price:** $_____
23"   (b) **Financing Terms:** ☐ Cash ☐ Conventional ☐ VA ☐ FHA ☐ Other (specify) _____
24"   ☐ **Seller** Financing: **Seller** will hold a purchase money mortgage in the amount of $_____
25"   with the following terms: _____
26"   ☐ Assumption of Existing Mortgage: Buyer may assume existing mortgage for $_____ plus
27"   an assumption fee of $_____. The mortgage is for a term of _____ years beginning in
28"   _____, at an interest rate of _____ % ☐ fixed ☐ variable (describe) _____
29"   Lender approval of assumption ☐ is required ☐ is not required ☐ unknown. **Notice to Seller:** (1) You may
30   remain liable for an assumed mortgage for a number of years after the Property is sold. Check with your
31   lender to determine the extent of your liability. **Seller** will ensure that all mortgage payments and required
32   escrow deposits are current at the time of closing and will convey the escrow deposit to the buyer at closing.
33   (2) Extensive regulations affect **Seller** financed transactions. It is beyond the scope of a real estate licensee's
34   authority to determine whether the terms of your **Seller** financing agreement comply with all applicable laws or
35   whether you must be registered and/or licensed as a loan originator before offering **Seller** financing. You are
36   advised to consult with a legal or mortgage professional to make this determination.
37"   (c) **Seller Expenses:** **Seller** will pay mortgage discount or other closing costs not to exceed _____ % of the
38   purchase price and any other expenses **Seller** agrees to pay in connection with a transaction.

39 4. **Broker Obligations:** **Broker** agrees to make diligent and continued efforts to sell the Property in accordance with
40   this Agreement until a sales contract is pending on the Property.

41 5. **Multiple Listing Service:** Placing the Property in a multiple listing service (the "MLS") is beneficial to **Seller**
42   because the Property will be exposed to a large number of potential buyers. As a MLS participant, **Broker** is
43   obligated to enter the Property into the MLS within one (1) business day of marketing the Property to the public
44   (see Paragraph 6(a)) or as necessary to comply with local MLS rule(s). This listing will be published accordingly in
45   the MLS unless **Seller** directs **Broker** otherwise in writing. (See paragraph 6(b)(i)). **Seller** authorizes **Broker** to
46   report to the MLS this listing information and price, terms, and financing information on any resulting sale for use
47   by authorized Board / Association members and MLS participants and subscribers unless **Seller** directs **Broker**
48   otherwise in writing.

Exclusive Right of Sale Listing Agreement

FloridaRealtors®

1   This Exclusive Right of Sale Listing Agreement ("Agreement") is between

2"   _____John Doe_____ ("**Seller**")

3"   and _____Your Real Estate Company_____ ("**Broker**").

4   **1. Authority to Sell Property: Seller** gives **Broker** the EXCLUSIVE RIGHT TO SELL the real and personal
5   property (collectively "Property") described below, at the price and terms described below, beginning
6"   _____March 1, 2022_____ and terminating at 11:59 p.m. on _____August 31, 2022_____ ("Termination Date"). Upon
7   full execution of a contract for sale and purchase of the Property, all rights and obligations of this Agreement will
8   automatically extend through the date of the actual closing of the sales contract. **Seller** and **Broker** acknowledge
9   that this Agreement does not guarantee a sale. This Property will be offered to any person without regard to race,
10   color, religion, sex, handicap, familial status, national origin, or any other factor protected by federal, state, or local
11   law. **Seller** certifies and represents that she/he/it is legally entitled to convey the Property and all improvements.

12   **2. Description of Property:**
13"   (a) **Street Address:** 123 Main Street, Miami, Florida 33111

14

15"   Legal Description: and#xA4;GRAND CANAL SUB PB 100-00 Lot 1 BLK 1 LOT SIZE 70.000 X 100 OR 12345-6
16"   OR 12345-1234 1234 5_____ ☐ See Attachment _____

17"   (b) **Personal Property, including appliances:** _____Refrigerator, washer, dryer, stove, microwave, fan_____
18"   ☐ See Attachment _____

19   (c) **Occupancy:**
20"   Property ☒ is ☐ is not currently occupied by a tenant. If occupied, the lease term expires _March 15, 2022_.

21   **3. Price and Terms:** The property is offered for sale on the following terms or on other terms acceptable to **Seller**:
22"   (a) **Price:** $400,000.00
23"   (b) **Financing Terms:** ☒ Cash ☒ Conventional ☒ VA ☒ FHA ☐ Other (specify) _____
24"   ☐ **Seller** Financing: **Seller** will hold a purchase money mortgage in the amount of $_____
25"   with the following terms: _____
26"   ☐ Assumption of Existing Mortgage: Buyer may assume existing mortgage for $_____ plus
27"   an assumption fee of $_____. The mortgage is for a term of _____ years beginning in
28"   _____, at an interest rate of _____ % ☐ fixed ☐ variable (describe) _____.
29"   Lender approval of assumption ☐ is required ☐ is not required ☐ unknown. **Notice to Seller:** (1) You may
30   remain liable for an assumed mortgage for a number of years after the Property is sold. Check with your
31   lender to determine the extent of your liability. **Seller** will ensure that all mortgage payments and required
32   escrow deposits are current at the time of closing and will convey the escrow deposit to the buyer at closing.
33   (2) Extensive regulations affect **Seller** financed transactions. It is beyond the scope of a real estate licensee's
34   authority to determine whether the terms of your **Seller** financing agreement comply with all applicable laws or
35   whether you must be registered and/or licensed as a loan originator before offering **Seller** financing. You are
36   advised to consult with a legal or mortgage professional to make this determination.
37"   (c) **Seller Expenses: Seller** will pay mortgage discount or other closing costs not to exceed _____ % of the
38   purchase price and any other expenses **Seller** agrees to pay in connection with a transaction.

39   **4. Broker Obligations: Broker** agrees to make diligent and continued efforts to sell the Property in accordance with
40   this Agreement until a sales contract is pending on the Property.

41   **5. Multiple Listing Service:** Placing the Property in a multiple listing service (the "MLS") is beneficial to **Seller**
42   because the Property will be exposed to a large number of potential buyers. As a MLS participant, **Broker** is
43   obligated to enter the Property into the MLS within one (1) business day of marketing the Property to the public
44   (see Paragraph 6(a)) or as necessary to comply with local MLS rule(s). This listing will be published accordingly in
45   the MLS unless **Seller** directs **Broker** otherwise in writing. (See paragraph 6(b)(i)). **Seller** authorizes **Broker** to
46   report to the MLS this listing information and price, terms, and financing information on any resulting sale for use
47   by authorized Board / Association members and MLS participants and subscribers unless **Seller** directs **Broker**
48   otherwise in writing.

(39)4. Broker obligations: from the broker/agent to the seller for the sale of the property.

(41)5. Multiple Listing Service: Notify the seller that you will place the property on the MLS and how the seller will benefit from this service. If sellers disagree, they need to initial that they do not want to place the property on the MLS.

Exclusive Right to Lease Agreement

This agreement is used for all types of residential rentals. It could be for a house, condo, mobile home, duplex, triplex, or fourplex. Realtors who specialize in working with landlords have good recurring income every renewal period. In addition, every time a tenant leaves, it's possible to do another lease agreement if you keep your client happy.

Have everything ready before you visit the landlord or owner: the CMA, IMAPP, and any other documentation you would like to use. If you will be doing a virtual appointment, have everything ready on your computer so it's easy to share documents with the owner.

This agreement is between the owner of the property and the broker agency.

On the first two lines, add the owner's name and on line two your company name.

1. Authority to lease property: write the beginning date of the listing and the ending date of the listing. In lease listing, this does not need to be a long time because usually if the price is right the listing will not last. Your range should be no less than 30 days and the maximum will depend on the price. For an average rental price, this should be at least two months, while a luxury rental will take more time.

2. Description of property: print it out or have the IMAPP (tax data) handy to fill out this section.

(a) Address, and (b) legal description; (c) ☐ check the occupancy, if it ☐ is not occupied or ☐ occupied and by whom? Include when the existing lease will expire: _____. It is important to ask when the lease expires so as not to have any surprises.

3. Rental rate and terms:

(a) Rental period and rate: choose the box ☐ that applies to your client. In a year lease, the amount the tenant will pay each month, check ☐ monthly and the amount $_____.

(b) Advance rent, deposits, and fees: check who will hold the tenant's deposit. Usually, check ☐ owner unless your company holds escrow accounts and manages rental properties. Check the box that says non-interest-bearing account unless the owners want to check the other boxes.

Exclusive Right to Lease Listing Agreement

FloridaRealtors

This Exclusive Right to Lease Listing Agreement ("Agreement") is between

_____ ("Owner") and

_____ ("Broker")

1. AUTHORITY TO LEASE PROPERTY: Owner gives **Broker** the EXCLUSIVE RIGHT TO SECURE A TENANT for the real and personal property ("Property") described below beginning the _____, and ending at 11:59 p.m. the _____ ("Listing Period"). If the Property becomes vacant during the Listing Period, **Owner** and **Broker** remain obligated to perform under this Agreement until the Listing Period expires. **Owner** certifies and represents that he/she is legally entitled to lease the Property.

2. DESCRIPTION OF PROPERTY:
    (a) Real Property: Street address: _____
        Legal Description: _____
    (b) Personal property, including appliances: _____
    _____
    _____

    (c) Occupancy: Property ☐ is not currently occupied ☐ is currently occupied by ☐ Landlord ☐ Tenant. If tenant occupied, the lease term expires: _____

3. RENTAL RATE AND TERMS:
    (a) **Rental Period and Rate:** ☐ Yearly $_____ ☐ Monthly $_____ ☐ Weekly $_____
    ☐ Seasonally $_____ "Season" runs from _____ to _____
    Specify any services or fees such as water, garbage, association dues, etc., that are included in rent: _____
    _____

    (b) **Advanced Rents, Deposits and Fees:** Advanced rents and deposits will be held by ☐ **Owner** ☐ **Broker** in a Florida financial institution, if required by Florida Landlord and Tenant law, in a(n)
        ☐ non-interest bearing account.
        ☐ interest-bearing escrow account, tenant to receive 5% per year, simple interest. Any balance of interest will accrue to ☐ **Owner** ☐ **Broker**
        ☐ interest-bearing escrow account, tenant to receive _____% (at least 75%) per year of the annualized average interest rate payable on the account. Any balance of interest will accrue to ☐ **Owner** ☐ **Broker.**
    ☐ Advanced rent $_____ ☐ Security Deposit: $_____
    ☐ Pet deposit ☐ refundable ☐ nonrefundable $_____
    ☐ Credit Report Fee: $_____ ☐ Other: _____ : $_____
    ☐ Association Application Fee: $_____ ☐ Other: _____ : $_____

    (c) **Taxes:** Leases for a term of 6 months or less are subject to state tax on transient rentals and to local tax on tourist development and impact. The party who receives the rent is responsible for timely collecting and remitting said taxes.

    (d) **Association Approval:** Application must be made (when) _____

4. BROKER OBLIGATIONS: In consideration of **Owner's** agreement to enter into this Agreement, **Broker** agrees to use: diligent effort to lease the Property; furnish information to and assist cooperating brokers in negotiating leases; furnish information to and assist attorneys when needed to draft leases; negotiate leases and renewals of existing leases in accordance with the rent schedule and terms above; take reasonable precautions to prevent damage to the Property when the Property is being shown by **Broker** or any other broker or sales associate; and to perform the following activities authorized by **Owner (check if applicable):**
    ☐ Display appropriate transaction signs, including a "For Rent" sign, on the Property.
    ☐ Use **Owner's** name in connection with marketing or advertising the Property.
    ☐ Use a lockbox system to access and show the Property.
    ☐ Request a credit check on prospective tenants at **Owner's** expense. **Broker** makes no representations as to the truth or falsity of information provided by the prospective tenant or as to the financial integrity or fitness and character of the prospective tenant.
    ☐ Execute leases on behalf of **Owner** (**Owner** must execute a Special Power of Attorney authorizing **Broker** to lease Property on **Owner's** behalf).
    ☐ Compensate any subagents or cooperating brokers in the transaction, except when not in **Owner's** best interest.
    ☐ Withhold offers to lease Property once **Owner** enters into a binding lease agreement.
    ☐ Make a final inspection and inventory check of Property at conclusion of lease.
    ☐ Complete lease forms as permitted by law.
    ☐ Complete and sign the lead-based paint/hazards certification on Owner's behalf (for Property built before 1978).
    ☐ Other _____

Owner (____) (____) and **Broker/Sales Associate** (____) (____) acknowledge receipt of a copy of this page, which is Page 1 of 4 Pages.

ERL-11   Rev 3/21
Serial# 073687-000164-5140838

©2021 Florida Realtors®
Form Simplicity

Exclusive Right to Lease Listing Agreement

FloridaRealtors®

This Exclusive Right to Lease Listing Agreement ("Agreement") is between

_____ John Doe _____ ("Owner") and

_____ Your Real Estate Company _____ ("Broker")

1. AUTHORITY TO LEASE PROPERTY: Owner gives **Broker** the EXCLUSIVE RIGHT TO SECURE A TENANT for the real and personal property ("Property") described below beginning the _____ 1 day of March, 2022 _____, and ending at 11:59 p.m. the _____ 31 day of May, 2022 _____ ("Listing Period"). If the Property becomes vacant during the Listing Period, **Owner** and **Broker** remain obligated to perform under this Agreement until the Listing Period expires. **Owner** certifies and represents that he/she is legally entitled to lease the Property.

2. DESCRIPTION OF PROPERTY:
   (a) Real Property: Street address: _____ 123 Main Street, Miami, Florida 33111 _____
   Legal Description: _____ and#xA4;GRAND CANAL SUB PB 100-00 Lot 1 BLK 1 LOT SIZE 70.000 X 100 OR 12345-678 9101 2 _____
   (b) Personal property, including appliances: _____ Washer, Dryer, Refrigerator, Stove _____

   (c) Occupancy: Property ☐ is not currently occupied ☒ is currently occupied by ☒ Landlord ☐ Tenant. If tenant occupied, the lease term expires: _____

3. RENTAL RATE AND TERMS:
   (a) **Rental Period and Rate:** ☐ Yearly $_____ ☒ Monthly $ 2,500.00 _____ ☐ Weekly $_____
   ☐ Seasonally $_____ "Season" runs from _____ to _____
   Specify any services or fees such as water, garbage, association dues, etc., that are included in rent: Association dues

   (b) **Advanced Rents, Deposits and Fees:** Advanced rents and deposits will be held by ☒ **Owner** ☐ **Broker** in a Florida financial institution, if required by Florida Landlord and Tenant law, in a(n)
      ☒ non-interest bearing account.
      ☐ interest-bearing escrow account, tenant to receive 5% per year, simple interest. Any balance of interest will accrue to ☐ **Owner** ☐ **Broker**
      ☐ interest-bearing escrow account, tenant to receive _____ % (at least 75%) per year of the annualized average interest rate payable on the account. Any balance of interest will accrue to ☐ **Owner** ☐ **Broker**.
      ☒ Advanced rent $ 2,500.00 _____ ☒ Security Deposit: $ 2,500.00 _____
      ☒ Pet deposit ☒ refundable ☐ nonrefundable $ 100.00 _____
      ☐ Credit Report Fee: $ _____ ☒ Other: Last month : $ 2,500.00
      ☒ Association Application Fee: $ 100.00 ☐ Other: _____ : $ _____

   (c) **Taxes:** Leases for a term of 6 months or less are subject to state tax on transient rentals and to local tax on tourist development and impact. The party who receives the rent is responsible for timely collecting and remitting said taxes.
   (d) **Association Approval:** Application must be made (when) _____ execute lease _____ .

4. BROKER OBLIGATIONS: In consideration of **Owner's** agreement to enter into this Agreement, **Broker** agrees to use: diligent effort to lease the Property; furnish information to and assist cooperating brokers in negotiating leases; furnish information to and assist attorneys when needed to draft leases; negotiate leases and renewals of existing leases in accordance with the rent schedule and terms above; take reasonable precautions to prevent damage to the Property when the Property is being shown by **Broker** or any other broker or sales associate; and to perform the following activities authorized by **Owner (check if applicable):**
      ☒ Display appropriate transaction signs, including a "For Rent" sign, on the Property.
      ☐ Use **Owner's** name in connection with marketing or advertising the Property.
      ☒ Use a lockbox system to access and show the Property.
      ☐ Request a credit check on prospective tenants at **Owner's** expense. **Broker** makes no representations as to the truth or falsity of information provided by the prospective tenant or as to the financial integrity or fitness and character of the prospective tenant.
      ☐ Execute leases on behalf of **Owner** (**Owner** must execute a Special Power of Attorney authorizing **Broker** to lease Property on **Owner's** behalf).
      ☒ Compensate any subagents or cooperating brokers in the transaction, except when not in **Owner's** best interest.
      ☐ Withhold offers to lease Property once **Owner** enters into a binding lease agreement.
      ☐ Make a final inspection and inventory check of Property at conclusion of lease.
      ☒ Complete lease forms as permitted by law.
      ☐ Complete and sign the lead-based paint/hazards certification on Owner's behalf (for Property built before 1978).
      ☐ Other _____

Owner (____) (____) and **Broker/Sales Associate** (____) (____) acknowledge receipt of a copy of this page, which is Page 1 of 4 Pages.

Click all the ☐ boxes that apply to the rental such as ☐ advance rent, ☐ security deposit, ☐ pet deposit if the owner accepts pets and if they will ask for a deposit, and if the pet deposit is refundable or nonrefundable. The last month's rent should be in any box that say other: _____ Last month $ _____. If there is any association, check the association application fee $ _____

Ask about all the information related to the association, including any additional deposits, any restrictions or requirements, and how long it will take to be approved. If they have an application handy, you can upload it to the MLS to make it easier for the tenant agents to access.

(c) Let the owners know that if they rent for less than six months, they are subject to a tax on transient rentals.

(d) Write when the application must be made _____

4. Broker obligation: This part checks all the ☐ box(es) applicable to the obligation that you will perform as a broker/agent.

*The owner and broker/sales associate should initial each page.

Contract to Lease

This is not a lease agreement, and an actual lease should be signed before occupancy. The lease could be prepared by the listing agent or tenant agent with the form approved by Florida Realtors, an attorney, or the landlord

1. Parties: _____ Landlord/company name
   And _____ Tenant/company name
Agree to execute a lease agreement no later than the agreement date.
Who will prepare the lease? ☐ Landlord ☐ Tenant (If you leave it blank, the landlord will prepare the lease.)

2. Deposit: Who will hold the deposit? It could be the landlord, title company, or real estate company. The tenant has paid $ _____ to _____ [deposit holder]. This deposit will be transferred according to the landlord's instructions (according to paragraph 5) after the execution of the lease by both parties.

3. Property address: _____
Check the box if the property is ☐ furnished or ☐ unfurnished. If the property is furnished or partially furnished, the agent must attach an inventory of all furniture.
Add the following person to the tenants who will occupy the property. Ex: add the name of the spouse and children.

4. Lease term: Begins on _____ [date] and ends on _____ [date]. Always end the day before you start the lease. For example: 01/01/2022 to 12/31/2022.

5. Money due before occupancy: the tenant will pay the sum of $ _____ before occupying the property. The tenant will not be entitled to occupy the property or ask for the key before paying this amount.   '

First month rent $ _____ due _____

Advance rent for months of _____ $ _____ due _____

This only applies when the tenant pays more than the standard. Example: The second month, any month's rent more than the first, last, and security deposit.

Last month rent $ _____ due _____ (could be a specific date or date of walkthrough).

Security deposit $ _____ due _____ (could be a specific date or date of walkthrough).

Security deposit for association $ _____ due _____ (could be a specific date or date of walkthrough).

Some associations request a security deposit in addition to the landlord's security deposit.

Pet deposit $ _____ due _____ (could be a specific date or date of walkthrough).

See MLS if this security deposit will be refundable.

Other: _____ $ _____ due _____ (could be a specific date or date of walkthrough).

Add any other fees relating to the contract to lease. Ex: Landlord background and credit check, real estate company processing fee.

*The paragraph 2 Deposit will be credited as follows: (check as applicable) Just ☐ check each one that will be applied to the lease.

*If left blank, the deposit will be credited to the first month's rent. The remaining will be 1) security deposit, 2) last month's rent, 3) advance rent.

6. Rent payments, taxes, and charges: The total rent for the lease (if it is a 12-month lease, multiply the monthly rent times 12) $ _____ (excluding taxes). Only if applicable, tenant will pay taxes in the amount of $ _____

Check one of the ☐ boxes:

☐ in full on _____ [date] amount $ _____ (full lease paid upfront)

☐ monthly, on the ___ day (the first day of the month if left blank) in the amount of $ _____; fill out the date the tenant will pay if it is not the first of the month.

7. Pets: ☐ prohibited ☐ permitted, as described _____.

8. Smoking: ☐ prohibited ☐ permitted

All parties must initial the agreement (landlord and tenant), and sign and date it at the end. Include the email, phone number, and address of the tenant on the last page.

Contract to Lease

(This is not a Lease. A Lease should be signed before occupancy.)

🏠 FloridaRealtors®

1. **Parties:** _____ (Prospective "**Landlord**")
   and _____ (Prospective "**Tenant**")
   agree to execute a lease agreement ("Lease") no later than _____ [date] for the property described below. The Lease will include the terms set forth in Paragraphs 3-12 of this Contract to Lease ("Contract") and other mutually agreeable terms. ☐ **Landlord** ☐ **Tenant** (**Landlord** if left blank) will prepare the Lease.

2. **Deposit:** With the intention of entering into a Lease with **Landlord**, **Tenant** has paid $_____ ("Deposit") to _____ [deposit holder].
   Upon execution of a Lease by both parties, the parties authorize the deposit holder to transfer the Deposit according to **Landlord's** instructions, and **Landlord** will credit the Deposit to the money due under Paragraph 5 below.

3. **Property Address:** _____
   _____

   The property will be ☐ unfurnished ☐ furnished (attach inventory).
   The property will be used for only residential purposes and occupied by only **Tenant** and the following persons:
   _____

4. **Lease Term:** The Lease will begin on _____ [date] and end on _____ [date].

5. **Money Due before Occupancy: Tenant** will pay the sum of $_____ in accordance with this paragraph before occupying the property. **Tenant** will not be entitled to move in or to keys to the property until all money due before occupancy has been paid. If no date is specified below, then funds will be due before occupancy.

First month's rent plus applicable taxes	$_____	due _____
Advance rent for month of _____ plus applicable taxes	$_____	due _____
Last month's rent plus applicable taxes	$_____	due _____
Security deposit	$_____	due _____
Security deposit for Association	$_____	due _____
Pet deposit	$_____	due _____
Other: _____	$_____	due _____
Other: _____	$_____	due _____

   The Paragraph 2 Deposit will be credited as follows: (**Check as applicable**)

   ☐ $_____ to first month's rent   ☐ $_____ to security deposit
   ☐ $_____ to last month's rent   ☐ $_____ other (specify) _____

   (If left blank, the Deposit will be credited to the first month's rent. Any remaining balance will be credited to the amounts due in the following order: 1) security deposit, 2) last month's rent, and 3) advance rent.)

6. **Rent Payments, Taxes, and Charges: Tenant** will pay total rent for the Lease Term of $_____ (excluding taxes). **Tenant** will also pay total taxes on the rent when applicable in the amount of $_____.
   Tenant will pay the rent, including taxes when applicable, as follows: (**Check one**)
   ☐ in full on _____ [date] in the amount of $_____.
   ☐ monthly, on the _____ day (the 1st day if left blank) of each month in the amount of $_____.

7. **Pets:** ☐ prohibited ☐ permitted, as described _____

8. **Smoking:** ☐ prohibited ☐ permitted

Prospective Tenant (_____) (_____) and Prospective Landlord (_____) (_____) acknowledge receipt of a copy of this page, which is Page 1 of 3.

Contract to Lease
(This is not a Lease. A Lease should be signed before occupancy.)

⟨Ŷ⟩ FloridaRealtors

1. **Parties:** _____ John Doe _____ (Prospective **"Landlord"**)
and _____ Mary Smith _____ (Prospective **"Tenant"**)
agree to execute a lease agreement ("Lease") no later than _____ March 14, 2022 _____ [date] for the property described below. The Lease will include the terms set forth in Paragraphs 3-12 of this Contract to Lease ("Contract") and other mutually agreeable terms. ☒ **Landlord** ☐ **Tenant** (**Landlord** if left blank) will prepare the Lease.

2. **Deposit:** With the intention of entering into a Lease with **Landlord**, **Tenant** has paid $2,500.00 _____ ("Deposit")
to _____ Any Realty Inc _____ [deposit holder].
Upon execution of a Lease by both parties, the parties authorize the deposit holder to transfer the Deposit according to **Landlord's** instructions, and **Landlord** will credit the Deposit to the money due under Paragraph 5 below.

3. **Property Address:** 123 Main Street, Miami, Florida 33111 _____
_____

   The property will be ☒ unfurnished ☐ furnished (attach inventory).
   The property will be used for only residential purposes and occupied by only **Tenant** and the following persons:
   Mary Doe

4. **Lease Term:** The Lease will begin on _____ April 1, 2022 _____ [date] and end on _____ March 31, 2023 _____ [date].

5. **Money Due before Occupancy:** **Tenant** will pay the sum of $7,500.00 _____ in accordance with this paragraph before occupying the property. **Tenant** will not be entitled to move in or to keys to the property until all money due before occupancy has been paid. If no date is specified below, then funds will be due before occupancy.

First month's rent plus applicable taxes	$ 2,500.00 due	upon acceptance
Advance rent for month of _____ plus applicable taxes	$ _____ due	_____
Last month's rent plus applicable taxes	$ 2,500.00 due	April 1, 2022
Security deposit	$ 2,500.00 due	April 1, 2022
Security deposit for Association	$ _____ due	_____
Pet deposit	$ _____ due	_____
Other: _____	$ _____ due	_____
Other: _____	$ _____ due	_____

The Paragraph 2 Deposit will be credited as follows. (**Check as applicable**)

☒ $2,500.00 _____ to first month's rent   ☒ $2,500.00 _____ to security deposit
☒ $2,500.00 _____ to last month's rent   ☐ $ _____ other (specify) _____

(If left blank, the Deposit will be credited to the first month's rent. Any remaining balance will be credited to the amounts due in the following order: 1) security deposit, 2) last month's rent, and 3) advance rent.)

6. **Rent Payments, Taxes, and Charges:** **Tenant** will pay total rent for the Lease Term of $30,000.00 _____ (excluding taxes). **Tenant** will also pay total taxes on the rent when applicable in the amount of $ _____ .
Tenant will pay the rent, including taxes when applicable, as follows: (**Check one**)
☐ in full on _____ [date] in the amount of $ _____ .
☒ monthly, on the _1_ day (the 1st day if left blank) of each month in the amount of $2,500.00 _____ .

7. **Pets:** ☒ prohibited ☐ permitted, as described _____

8. **Smoking:** ☒ prohibited ☐ permitted

Prospective Tenant (____) (____) and Prospective Landlord (____) (____) acknowledge receipt of a copy of this page, which is Page 1 of 3.

Residential Lease for Single Family Home or Duplex

(For a Term Not to Exceed One Year)

When you see a ☐ box or a () blank space, it means a decision must be made by the parties.

1. The parties to the lease; this is a lease (the "Lease") between (name and address of landlord _____ _____ ("Landlord) and (tenant's name) _____ ("Tenant")

Fill in the landlord and tenant's email and phone number.

2. Property rented: Located at _____

List all furniture and appliances included (if none, write "none"); For example: refrigerator, stove, washer, dryer _____

List all people who will occupy the property. Example: spouse, children (list their names)

_____

3. Term: (not to exceed twelve months) beginning on _____ and ending _____ (the "Lease Term")

4. Rent payment, taxes, and charges: amount of the total lease term (multiply the monthly rent times the number of months of the lease, not to exceed 12 months, excluding taxes): $ _____

Choose if the tenant will pay in installments or in full:

☐ In installments:

    ☐ Monthly on the _____ day of each month (if left blank, on the first day of each month). If it's not the first day of the month, be sure to specify which day it will be. In the amount of $ _____ per installment.

    ☐ Weekly on the _____ day of each week (if left blank, every Monday of each week) in the amount of $ _____ per installment

☐ In full on (date) _____ in the amount of $ _____. (Use this one only if the tenant will pay the full lease upfront.)

Residential Lease for Single Family Home or Duplex
(FOR A TERM NOT TO EXCEED ONE YEAR)

FloridaRealtors®

A BOX (☐) OR A BLANK SPACE (____) INDICATES A PROVISION WHERE A CHOICE OR DECISION MUST BE MADE BY THE PARTIES.

THE LEASE IMPOSES IMPORTANT LEGAL OBLIGATIONS. MANY RIGHTS AND RESPONSIBILITIES OF THE PARTIES ARE GOVERNED BY CHAPTER 83, PART II, RESIDENTIAL LANDLORD AND TENANT ACT, FLORIDA STATUTES. A COPY OF THE RESIDENTIAL LANDLORD AND TENANT ACT IS ATTACHED TO THIS LEASE.

1. **PARTIES.** This is a lease (the "Lease") between _____
(name and address of owner of the property)

_____ ("Landlord") and

_____
(name(s) of person(s) to whom the property is leased)

_____ ("Tenant").

Landlord's E-mail Address: _____

Landlord's Telephone Number: _____

Tenant's E-mail Address: _____

Tenant's Telephone Number: _____

2. **PROPERTY RENTED.** Landlord leases to Tenant the land and buildings located at _____
(street address)

_____, Florida _____
(zip code)

together with the following furniture and appliances [List all furniture and appliances. If none, write "none."] (In the Lease, the property leased, including furniture and appliances, if any, is called the "Premises"):

_____

_____

The Premises shall be occupied only by the Tenant and the following persons: _____

_____

3. **TERM.** This is a lease for a term, not to exceed twelve months, beginning on _____ and
(month, day, year)
ending _____ (the "Lease Term").
(month, day, year)

4. **RENT PAYMENTS, TAXES AND CHARGES.** Tenant shall pay total rent in the amount of $_____ (excluding taxes) for the Lease Term. The rent shall be payable by Tenant in advance in installments or in full as provided in the options below:

☐ in installments. If in installments, rent shall be payable

☐ monthly, on the _____ day of each month (if left blank, on the first day of each month) in the amount of $_____ per installment.

OR

☐ weekly, on the _____ day of each week (If left blank, on Monday of each week.) in the amount of $_____ per installment.

☐ in full on _____ in the amount of $_____.
(date)

Tenant (____) (____) and Landlord (____) (____) acknowledge receipt of a copy of this page, which is Page 1 of 18.

RLHD-3x   Rev 7/16   Approved on April 15, 2010, by the Supreme Court of Florida, for use under rule 10-2.1(a) of the Rules Regulating the Florida Bar.
Serial#: 049390-300164-5142486

Form Simplicity

THE PRODUCTIVE AGENT

Residential Lease for Single Family Home or Duplex
(FOR A TERM NOT TO EXCEED ONE YEAR)

FloridaRealtors®

A BOX (☐) OR A BLANK SPACE (___) INDICATES A PROVISION WHERE A CHOICE OR DECISION MUST BE MADE BY THE PARTIES.

THE LEASE IMPOSES IMPORTANT LEGAL OBLIGATIONS. MANY RIGHTS AND RESPONSIBILITIES OF THE PARTIES ARE GOVERNED BY CHAPTER 83, PART II, RESIDENTIAL LANDLORD AND TENANT ACT, FLORIDA STATUTES. A COPY OF THE RESIDENTIAL LANDLORD AND TENANT ACT IS ATTACHED TO THIS LEASE.

1. PARTIES. This is a lease (the "Lease") between _____ John Doe _____
(name and address of owner of the property)

_____ ("Landlord") and

Mary Smith
(name(s) of person(s) to whom the property is leased)

_____ ("Tenant").

Landlord's E-mail Address: landlord@gmail.com

Landlord's Telephone Number: 305-111-2222

Tenant's E-mail Address: tenant@gmail.com

Tenant's Telephone Number: 305-222-3333

2. PROPERTY RENTED. Landlord leases to Tenant the land and buildings located at ___ 123 Main Ave ___
(street address)

Your city , Florida 33111
(zip code)

together with the following furniture and appliances [List all furniture and appliances. If none, write "none."] (In the Lease, the property leased, including furniture and appliances, if any, is called the "Premises"):

Refrigerator, fan, stove, washer, dryer

The Premises shall be occupied only by the Tenant and the following persons: Mary Doe

3. TERM. This is a lease for a term, not to exceed twelve months, beginning on ___ April 1, 2022 ___ and
(month, day, year)
ending ___ March 31, 2023 ___ (the "Lease Term").
(month, day, year)

4. RENT PAYMENTS, TAXES AND CHARGES. Tenant shall pay total rent in the amount of $30,000.00 (excluding taxes) for the Lease Term. The rent shall be payable by Tenant in advance in installments or in full as provided in the options below:

☒ in installments. If in installments, rent shall be payable

☒ monthly, on the ___1___ day of each month (if left blank, on the first day of each month) in the amount of $2,500.00 per installment.

OR

☐ weekly, on the _____ day of each week (If left blank, on Monday of each week.) in the amount of $_____ per installment.

☐ in full on _____ in the amount of $_____.
(date)

Tenant (___) (___) and Landlord (___) (___) acknowledge receipt of a copy of this page, which is Page 1 of 18.

RLHD-3x Rev 7/16 Approved on April 15, 2010, by the Supreme Court of Florida, for use under rule 10-2.1(a) of the Rules Regulating the Florida Bar.
Serial#: 061506-000164-5143025

Form Simplicity

112

Chapter 7

Real Estate Dictionary

A

Absentee Landlord: The lessor of a property who does not live on the property and seldom visits the property.

Absorption: Time it will take to rent or sell the unit compared to the overall supply of properties on the market.

Abstract: Summary of public record; recorded documents.

Accelerated Depreciation: Any type of method of depreciation that is faster to depreciate than the straight method.

Accessibility: In real estate could have several meanings. For example: accessibility that will pass the handicap accessibility requirements. Another is the ability of customers to reach a business location.

Access Right: Right of access to a property to ingress and egress. Could be expressed or implied.

Account Payable: Money owed. Could be service, liability. Represents an obligation.

Account Receivable: Abbreviation A/R or AR. Leases should maintain an account receivable. Money owed to a business for goods or services.

Accrual Accounting: Method of accounting that requires all payments to be recorded and incomes to be recorded when the transaction occurs.

Act of God: Known as mother nature. A natural disaster like a flood or hurricane.

Actual Eviction: Legal action to remove the tenant from the landlord's property and from the lease.

Addition: Adding something to the original structure. Example: A porch, a new room.

Additional Deposit: A second deposit in a sales transaction.

Adjacent: Next to another property.

Adjustable Rate Mortgage (ARM): Loan in which the interest rate fluctuates. Could adjust semi-annually or annually.

Adjusted Sales Price: Term used in appraisals to adjust the sales price to reflect the subject property price.

Adult: A person 18 years of age or older who can legally enter into a contract.

Agreement: All contracts are agreements. An agreement is between two or more people that lists obligations and rights to enforce something. Could be a sale, purchase, or service.

Allegation: Claim, declaration, statement, affirmation.

Alluvion: From the Latin "alluvium," an increase in land by natural causes on areas near the water.

Alterations: Changes in a property inside or outside without changing the exterior dimensions.

Amendment: Change, revision, or alteration of any part of the contract. A change for the better.

Amenities: The enhancement of a property that can be used by the tenant or property owner. Usually in condominium and homeowner associations, for example: a pool, golf course, or tennis court.

Amortize: The act of reducing a debt by paying payments to the principal and interest.

Annual: Yearly, some rents and memberships have the option for annual periods on the contract.

Annual Debt Service: The yearly annual payment of the debt service of principal and interest, usually calculated annually for mortgage loans.

Apartment: A unit in a building usually having one or more rooms. Rent can be short- or long-term.

Apartment Hotel: Also known as a condo hotel. These units are in a hotel and have all the amenities the hotel has. Can be rented seasonally or short-term.

Appraisal Method: There are three key methods: cost, income, and market value approach

Aqueduct: A conduit, channel, or watercourse to bring or carry water away.

Arable: Piece of land that is suitable for farming.

Arbitration Clause: Clause in a contract that stipulates future arbitration dispute processes.

Articles of Incorporation: General information about a company; filed in the state the corporation will be incorporated. Certificate of incorporation.

Asbestos: Fiber mineral material used in the construction of houses for insulation or exterior walls.

Assemblage: Collection, accumulation, group of two or more lots to put together to increase value.

Assessed Value: Determine the value of a property for property tax.

Assets: Everything the person or company owns that has value.

Assign: Transfer a property or right. Some tenants or buyers check assignment in the agreement in case the tenant or buyer wants to transfer the contract to another person or company.

Assignor: The person or entity who makes the assignment to transfer their property or right to another person or entity.

Associate Broker: Licensed real estate broker who chooses not to open their own real estate office and decides to work as a broker associate for another broker.

Attic: Space between the ceiling and the roof. Good for storage or to create another room.

Auction: Sale and purchase of goods or property through the bidding process. In real estate, the county court auctions multiple properties; some banks conduct auctions to sell their properties.

B

Back Title Letter: Letter given by the title company to an attorney (of the buyer or seller) to do a search from the date of the letter to check the title condition.

Back up Offer: A secondary offer to buy a property. Business that the seller agent keeps in case the first offer does not go through.

Balance Sheet: A statement that shows the assets and liabilities of a company or a person. Net worth.

Balcony: An enclosed platform usually on condos, townhouses, or the second floor of houses that is enclosed by walls or balustrades on the outside of a building usually with access from the interior of the property.

Balloon: Final payment of a mortgage or note.

Bankrupt: A person or entity that is unable to pay outstanding debts.

Basement: A room or rooms below the ground of a dwelling.

Base Rent: Minimum amount of rent before other expenses that will increase the rent payment.

Benchmark: Point of reference. Used in topographic surveys.

Betterment: Benefit, improvement of a property, land, an addition to the structure.

Bi: A prefix use for two, every two, like biannual.

Bid: An offer that competes with other offers. For example, a bid on a property for sale.

Bill of Sale: An instrument that transfers a property.

Biweekly Payment: A method that accelerates the payment of a mortgage debt to finish earlier than the loan term. Instead of paying monthly, people pay every two weeks to apply more to the principal.

Block: Square area in a city or county enclosed by streets. Used in some states as part of their legal description like block 1, lot 2, and so on.

Board: Group of people that the association authorizes by law to manage for the benefit of its members. Example: The board of realtors.

Breach of Warranty: When a seller fails to pass title.

Bulk Transfer: The sale of all properties in bulk, together, whole.

Builder: Company or person who manufactures or constructs structures.

Building Restrictions: Prohibited by government, city, or county to construct with certain types of materials or certain construction designs.

Bundle of Legal Rights: Legal privileges to a buyer through the purchase of a property. Possession control of all legal rights of land or property.

Business Cycle: Fluctuations in the price of business. The value of properties goes up and down depending on the cycle of expansion, recession, and reactivation. Also known as the property cycle from decline upward.

Business Opportunity: The sale of a business that usually does not include the real estate. It includes the business, customer lists, inventory, and the goodwill of the business.

C

Canal: Waterway channels or manmade artificial waterways to connect water, usually for irrigation or for other purposes.

Cap: Maximum amount charged for a service or loan.

Capital: Money a person has for investing to create income.

Carport: A roof made to park a car under to prevent sun exposure or rain damage.

Cash: Money and its equivalent (checks, notes, money order, etc.).

Cash Discount: A discount if the invoice is paid before a certain date.

Cashier's Check: A check that is acceptable at the time of closing a rental agreement or sale. The cashier's check does not need to wait to clear because it is not from an individual. It is normally issued by a bank.

Certificate: Writing instrument from a court or government with certain rights and obligations. Other examples: a real estate certificate, certificate of occupancy.

Certified Check: Like a cashier's check in terms of using it for closing because the funds are guaranteed by the bank. The bank sets aside the funds from the cashier's check to ensure the person does not spend the money in the bank account.

Chattel: Property, goods, immovable property (land or building).

Chattel Mortgage: A lien on a property.

City: A large town, municipal corporation.

Claim: A demand or right of something to have the right to claim. Could be due to negligence and later the other party can make a claim. A dispute.

Clearance: Any area that was not clean and is now clean. Action of removing or getting rid of trash.

Cluster Housing: Construction of buildings around a small yard as a common area for everyone in the development.

Collateral: Something that secures a loan. In a mortgage loan, the collateral is the property.

Commercial Property: Property designated by the city and/or county for business use as a commercial zone (restaurants, salon, banks, etc.).

Commitment: A promise that a bank gives to a person or entity that qualifies for a loan with the conditions and time set on the written document.

Competent: A person who is legally able to sign a legal document.

Comprehensive Plan: A general plan. A written document with goals, objectives, policies, and more for marketing, a service, or any other type of plan.

Conditional Use Permit: A temporary governmental permit used in necessary circumstances, such as for medical purposes (like a temporary vaccination center, etc.).

Conditions: Some condition that needs to be cleared before closing a real estate transaction, such as verification of employment or liens on the property.

Conditional Sale of Real Estate Property: When parties have sets of conditions before fulfilling the contract, such as securing financing or when another property needs to be sold first.

Consideration: Any form of value that can be used as a consideration, a deposit to a real estate contract.

Consolidation: In a mortgage, to consolidate two or more loans into one loan.

Contribution: In real estate, could be a seller's contribution for a buyer's closing cost. A contribution could be a service, action, or money.

Cooperative Apartment: Known as a co-op. A building of two or more units. It's harder to get a loan because ownership is a portion of stock in the cooperative.

Cost: Amount or equivalent paid for something such as a service or property.

Credit: Obtain goods or services before payment. In real estate, buying a property on credit with a mortgage.

Crop: Specific harvest in a specific season. Example: A corn crop.

Custodian: A person in charge of other individual's real and personal property as well as guardianship over that person.

Customer: In real estate, the buyer, consumer, or purchaser.

D

Doctrine of Relation Back: Irrevocable deposit for a transfer of title. Something done today is treated as if it were done earlier.

Data Plan: Data quote from a telecommunications company. Database of clients, commercial properties, analysis, properties.

Dated Date: A date of an executed agreement, document. Different from a date of record on any document.

DBA (Doing Business As): Trade name or fictitious business name in which a company works.

Dead End Street: Not a through street. Same entrance and exit. A street with no outlet.

Debtor: A person or institution who owns a debt.

Debt Services: The amount of money that is required to pay interest and principal expenses. Debt service coverage ratio.

Deck: Flat structure or surface extended across a ship or boat.

Decree: An official judgment of a court.

Default Judgment: The party in a court that fails to come to court will be in default.

Defendant: A person or entity who is sued or accused in a court by another party (person, group, or company).

Deferred Payments: Payments that begin sometime in the future. Example: During the Covid-19 pandemic, some banks deferred mortgage payments for 3, 6, or more months.

Deflation: The opposite of inflation. Prices of properties decrease.

Demographics: Statistics, census. Knowing about the population, their income, etc.

Density: The number of people occupying any area, building, commercial zone, etc.

DRE (Department of Real Estate): Department that regulates and governs real estate licenses of brokers and agents.

Depletion: Loss, reduction of assets, loss of assets.

Depression: The lowest cycle in a business. When the economy has a higher rate of unemployment.

Deterioration: Physical deterioration that occurs gradually through time.

Discount: Also called mortgage points. Change in discount rate.

Disbursement: A payment of money.

Dissolution: The termination of a contract or business.

Distress Sale: The sale of a property for less because the seller is under pressure to sell.

Domestic Corporation: A corporation formed and conducting business in the same state.

Domicile: A permanent home. For corporations, the corporation domicile is the entity's address.

Donor: A person who gives a gift. In real estate, the donor could be a family member who helps with closing costs.

Driveway: Private roadway to a house. Can be paved or unpaved.

Drywall Construction: Panel made of calcium sulfate dehydrate. Known as sheetrock. Used for interior walls.

E

Economic Obsolescence: When a property loses value due to external factors. Example: A fast-food restaurant is built next to your house which could reduce your home's value.

Encroachment: Any part of one property that intrudes into another property, such as a wall or fence.

Earnings: All money received from labor, services, or dividends from a company.

Economics: The study of wealth related to or based on production, distribution, and consumption. For example, studying personal finance, companies, government, and private sectors. Also, the study of micro and macro-economic processes.

Effective Age: Age of a structure calculated by the conditions of the building and not by the age the property was built.

Egress: Access and ability to move across the land of another owner.

Environment: Surroundings, the area around a property that could affect or increase the value of a property.

Equator: Imaginary planetary line. The equator divides the planet into northern and southern hemispheres. Starting point for measuring latitude and longitude.

Equipment: In real estate, the apparatus a person leaves on the property as part of the sale that could be attached or detached like a refrigerator, dishwasher, or chandelier.

Equity Purchase: A person who buys a company's equity or just the equity of a property with an assumable mortgage.

Error and Omission Insurance (E&O): Liability insurance that covers any mistakes and omissions an agent or broker commits in a real estate transaction. This insurance protects agents and brokers by providing legal defense.

Estate: A large piece of land on which to build a house. Examples are real estate or life estate (the estate of a deceased person, etc.).

Expansible House: A house that has the possibility of continuing to build on it in the future.

Expense Stop/Cap: Limit of expenses to not surpass the amount agreed upon, usually on commercial leases.

Expenses of Sale: All expenses related to the sale of a property such as mortgage points (if the seller contributes to a buyer's closing costs), closing costs, title fees, real estate taxes (documentary transfer state tax, etc.), real estate commissions, and more.

Exposure: In real estate, how the property is built on the lot: exposed to the east, west, south, or north.

Exterior: Any building or home exterior. The outside of a dwelling.

F

Face: The front exposure of a property. The façade.

Face Value: The value of a mortgage, notes, etc.

Fair Credit Reporting Act: The ability and right for a person or entity to see their credit report at no cost. They may write to the credit bureau to explain their credit report if they find any incorrect items on their report.

Fair Market Value: A fair price for a property based on a comparable market analysis in the area. The buyer and seller agree in a reasonable time and price to buy and sell the property.

False Advertisement: In real estate, incorrectly advertising the details of a property such as the terms, square feet, amenities, etc. If a broker continues doing this, they could lose their license.

Family Room: A room usually next to the kitchen that people use for family activities.

Farmers Home Administration: An organization established in 1946 for the benefit of farmers.

FDIC Federal Insurance Deposit Corporation: Agency that provides deposit insurance to depositors.

Federal Tax Lien: A lien recorded on a property when a person is delinquent on personal, state, property, or income tax, etc.

Fee: A charge for a service. Could be a real estate transaction fee, the cleaning fee for a property, and more.

Fence: Structure that encloses an area made of wood, posts, boards, wires, metal, etc. Could be the front, the whole property, the left or right side of the property, or the back of the property.

Fictitious Name: Also known as DBA (doing business as). The owner of the company files a fictitious name to work under this name (in Florida, on sunbiz.org), or via the corporation division in the state.

Financing Cost: All costs incurred in the financing or loan to purchase a property or business.

First Time Buyer: A buyer who has not yet purchased a residential property. Can use different programs to get a lower down payment like the FHA, Fannie Mae, or Community Home Buyer Program. There are several programs designed to help first time buyers.

Flat: Relating to a real estate commission, a flat fee for the transaction. Example: Brokers charge a flat fee for their service no matter the sales or rent price. Also, a flat surface, level, smooth.

Flood: An area of inundation of water, swamping.

Forgery: Fraudulent act to forge a signature or alter anything to commit any type of fraud.

Fractional Section: A parcel of land divided in sections that is less than 40 acres.

Funds: Related to customers in real estate, the available funds a person has for buying, renting, or to do a business transaction.

G

Gain: Profit from a sales transaction.

Garage: In a house, an enclosed area to park cars. In business, a structure for repairing cars, etc.

Garbage Disposal: A small electrical device installed in the sink to grind the garbage into small pieces.

Gazebo: Usually an open octagonal structure in the backyard of a house.

General Contractor: Person responsible for the overall construction who hires subcontracting personnel in areas such as electrical, plumbing, and more.

General Partner: The partner in the partnership who has the authority and responsibility for the actions of the business.

General Warranty Deed: The most used deed in a real estate sale transaction.

Gift: Transferring a property without a transfer of value. A gift at closing from the seller, a family (which must be disclosed in an addendum), or part of the broker commission (must also be disclosed in the real estate contract).

Goodwill: Mostly used on business opportunity sales, a transaction based on the reputation and good name of the business.

Grace Period: Used in any loan, lease, or insurance, the time a person can pay after the due date without penalty. Example: Rent is due the first of each month but usually has a maximum of five calendar days to pay without any penalties.

Graduated Lease: The lease varies based on the price in the area through an appraisal or with an agreement between the landlord and tenant.

Graduated Payment Mortgage (GPM): A graduated increment of the mortgage payment of the interest loan.

Gross: Total with no adjustments. Can be gross square feet, gross rent, gross income, etc.

Gross Income: The entire income a person or entity receives. Example: For self-employed, a 1099 form.

Ground Water: Water that is underground in a saturated zone, land surface.

H

Habendum: Clause in a deed that defines the property granted.

Habitable Room: Room in a house counted as a room such as bedrooms, kitchen, or living room.

Hacienda: A large estate or plantation with a house.

Hall: Narrow space between rooms and condos or apartments in a building.

Hard Money Mortgage: Usually these loans have a shorter term than the standard loans on a property. These loans are secured by a property and have a higher interest rate than conventional loans. Mostly issued by private investors.

Head of a Family-Head of Household: The person in charge of the family. Could be a spouse, a brother, sister, or child, etc. Person who supports one or more individuals who are related to him or her.

Heater: Device designed to warm a room or house. Could be small individual unit or central unit.

Highway Frontage: Property/land in front of a highway; good for business exposure.

Holding Escrow: Holding escrow could be for a short period or a long period and can be a complicated agreement. An escrow account designated to hold escrow before a closing transaction on a property. Holding escrow in a transaction for a period until the problem is solved; could be a lien on a property, a collection, a claim, etc.

Holdover Tenant: A renter that stays in the property after the lease agreement expires.

Homeowners Association: An association formed with a group of owners in the building, a complex to improve, clean, and maintain the place in good standing. Requires having a structure of rules and regulations, legal status in some states, and more.

Homestead Exception: Helps homeowners reduce taxes up to $50,000 in Florida from their tax bill. Additionally, help homeowners limit tax increases to a maximum cap per year of 3% under the Save Our Home (SOH) Act or a percentage change in the consumer price index.

Hypothecate: Give a property as a guarantee for a loan without giving possession of the estate.

I

Immovable: In real estate, land, houses, and buildings are considered permanent.

Implied: Implicit, insinuated, or suggested, but not a direct action.

Income: Money received as a return on investment or via a sale, labor, or work.

Income Property: A property that produces income through rent. Could be residential, commercial, multifamily, or partially owner occupied.

Incompetent: A person who cannot handle his/her property because of mental or physical health problem. The court designates a person who will administer the person's estate.

Incorporate: To unite or create a company or organization.

Increment: An increase in population, density, income, interest, payments, taxes, etc.

Independent Appraisal: An appraisal that an owner of a house pays for to find out the value of the property. Not used to change the interest rate of a loan, refinancing, or for sale.

Individual Retirement Account (IRA): A way to save money for individual retirement. The individual does not pay taxes until they take out the money, and they pay taxes at the individual tax bracket when the money is released. People can contribute up to a certain amount per year.

Industrial Property: Property or land with zoning for industrial purposes. Example: Heavy manufacturing building, warehouse, industrial park, etc.

Inheritance: Legacy, benefaction. Something that is inherited by law and not by will.

Initial: In real estate contracts, every page must be initialed by all the parties involved (buyer and seller, landlord and tenant, broker and owner). Additionally, if the agreement is changed all parties must date and initial each change.

Installment Sale: A sale with more than two payments and over two or more years. Financial arrangements between a seller and a buyer throughout a specific period.

Insulation: Helps decrease the amount of heat, cold, or sound in a property. Use between the walls, roof, etc.

Insurance: A guarantee from a company to compensate an individual or entity for specific damages, changes in property value, illness, death, or compensation in general.

Investment: The action of investing money in a property, improvement, etc., to get a positive return or profit.

J

Joint: Two or more people or companies that get together to form something such as joint tenancy, joint venture, etc.

Joint Appraisal: Two or more appraisals made by each appraiser. One of the appraisals will be the one that gets the price. Joint appraisal is common in court.

Joint Note: A promise to repay a debt that is executed by two or more parties.

Jointure: An estate that transfers to a wife for the period in which she survives her husband, in lieu of a dower.

Judgment Debtor: A person or entity against whom a judgment orders to pay. If the person or entity cannot pay, the person or entity may declare bankruptcy.

Judgment Lien: The court gives the creditor the right to go after the debtor's assets so they can get paid if the debtor fails to pay back their debts.

Judicial Foreclosure: Usually is administered by a sheriff via the county court. The person or entity that makes the highest offer buys the property. If no one bids on the property, the bank repossesses the property.

Judicial Sale: A sale ordered by a court. This is not a voluntary sale by the owner of the property. Example: The sale of a property pursuant to a foreclosure.

K

Keeper: A person who administers someone or something. A guardian or custodian.

Kilo: A prefix for kilometer, kilogram (1000 gram), one thousand.

Kilovolt: 1000 volts.

Kilowatts: A measurement of 1000 watts of electrical power.

Knoll: A small, rounded hill or mound.

L

Labor: Job, usually hard physical work. Example: A handyman job.

Laminate: Flat surface material with plastic, protective layers. Example: Laminated wood.

Land Bank: Banking association for the purpose of financing agricultural land, parcels, etc.

Land Contract: A contract paid in installments for the sale of land between the buyer and seller.

Land Grant: A gift of land from the federal government to a person, entity, state, city, or county.

Landlord Warrant: When a court gives the landlord authority to sell a tenant's personal property to gather delinquent rent, as well as possession of the property.

Landscape: Visible characteristics of a property, the land's aesthetic appeal. Picture that represents the view or scenery. Also, the orientation of a document in a printer.

Late Charge: A penalty imposed on the person or entity that does not pay on time. Example: A tenant should pay on the first of the month but goes past the five-day grace period. On the sixth of the month, they will pay a late fee.

Latitude: The distance north to south from the earth's equator.

Layout: The plan, design, arrangement, construction, and organization of something such as a property, land, or building.

Lease Hold Improvements: Improvements a tenant makes which the landlord agrees to remunerate. Also, a customized improvement or change for a tenant for a particular need.

Lender: The person, entity, bank, or investor that lends money.

Lessee: A tenant, the one who holds a lease on a property.

Lessor: A landlord, a person who leases a property.

Liable: Obligated, responsible for by law.

License: Permission to do something, permission to perform specific work. Issued by an authority like the state.

Licensee: The person who holds a license such as a real estate license or insurance license.

Loan: Institution or person lends money to someone.

Lobby: Open space for waiting, entrance of a building or hotels.

Love and Affection: Known in real estate as consideration. If you transfer a title of a deed to your son/daughter, then love and affection are consideration.

M

Made Land: Land artificially created, manmade. Improved or upgraded land to make more usable

Main: Large conduit or pipe that carries gas, sewer, etc.

Maker: Person or entity who creates; the signer of a note. Instrument that the maker assumes full responsibility for, such as a loan or agreement.

Marble: Hard rock limestone of diverse colors and designs used in construction for kitchens, floors, etc.

Marketability: The ability to sell and to advertise a property for sale.

Material Fact: Information that affects the sale of a building, property, or business. Example: A leak in the roof.

Meeting of the Minds: All parties agree to the terms. Example: In a real estate contract, a buyer asks the seller for a seller contribution and the seller agrees to the terms and price.

Merge: Two or more entities or individuals merge to form something bigger and better. Used in case only one of the individuals or companies survives; then, the other person or entity will continue.

Minimum Lot: Local zoning specified for the developer to build. The minimum lot size to build a house or other building.

Mistake: Unintentional error. In real estate, any mistake make by an agent or broker could result in a civil suit filed against them by the seller or buyer. Example: In the MLS, inputting a listing with an incorrect price, such as adding or forgetting a 0.

Monetary Policy: Policy in a country to regulate the interest rate and the nation's currency supply.

Monument: Visible mark that surveyors use to establish lines and boundaries.

Moratorium: A temporary prohibition, suspension, postponement, or freeze of an activity such as a delay in paying back a debt.

Mortgage Company: A firm that is licensed to originate real estate loans that can be residential or commercial; can charge fees for their services

Mortgage Insurance Premium (MIP): FHA and VA loans have an MIP for all loans with less than a 20% down payment. This insures the loans in case a buyer does not pay the loan; it protects the debt. This is an additional fee to the monthly payments.

Mortgage Servicing: Service of an existing mortgage. Lenders usually sell the servicing to another company that collects all payments including principal, interest, tax, and insurance. Then, the servicing company sends all the payments to the pertinent parties like insurance, county tax, and the lender.

Multifamily Dwelling: A dwelling for two or more families which could be apartments, duplexes, triplexes, or fourplexes.

N

Negative Cash Flow: Situation where a person or institution spends more money on the property or investment than it receives. In real estate, when an investor is losing money on an income property.

Non-Exclusive Listing: An open listing. The seller pays a commission only to the broker who supplies the buyer.

Name Change: When the title of a property is under an original name and the person changes their last name. The title must record both names.

Natural Person: A physical person, an individual human being.

Natural Resource: Reserves of resources such as minerals, oil, gold, etc.

Navigable: A waterway. Anything that is navigable can be sailed on by ship or boat such as a lake, the sea, or a river.

Negative Cash Flow: When an owner or entity's income is less than they are bringing in. Expenses are higher than income.

Negotiable: Used in some listings to tell other realtors that the price of the property can be negotiated; the sales price is not firm, and the seller is open to offers.

Net After Tax: The net income a property produces after paying taxes.

Net Before Tax: The net income of a property generated before paying income tax.

Net Income: Income minus expenses.

Net Worth: All assets minus all liabilities.

Nominal Consideration: Used on special contracts and not necessary money or actual value; could be little or no money. Example: A buyer buys a house for $100, when the property value is $100,000.

Non-Judicial Foreclosure Sale: A clause on a mortgage agreement that allows the lender to foreclose without the court's involvement.

Non-Profit Corporation: A corporation that has some tax and income tax exemption. Legal entity operating for a public or social benefit.

Nuisance: Person, thing, or circumstance that causes an annoyance. Example: An owner of a property is causing some type of noise that is inconvenient to other owners in the area.

O

Open-End Loan: A revolving line of credit. Example: A HELOC. The borrower can increase the loan amount up to the maximum.

Oath: An affirmation or promise to tell the truth. In court, witnesses place their hand on the Bible and swear to tell the truth.

Occupancy Rate: The ratio of rented units to vacant units in a building or complex.

Offer: A proposal or intention to buy or sell an asset with a specific price and terms.

Offsite Cost: Expenses related to construction.

Onsite Cost: Improvement cost of an onsite construction.

One Hour Fire Door: A door that is resistant to fire for at least one hour.

One Hour Fire Wall: A wall that is resistant to fire for at least one hour.

Open Mortgage: A mortgage with no pre-payment penalty.

Open Space Land: A land open and designed for parks or monuments. The city, county, and zoning office determines how it will be used.

Operating Expense: Ongoing costs for running a product, business, or system.

Optionee: The one who receives or buys an option. Recipient or holder of the option.

Optionor: The one who grants or sells an option.

Oral Contract: An agreement between two or more parties by spoken communication which may be partially written.

Origination Fee: A mortgage fee that companies, lenders, or banks charge to buyers for doing the loan. An origination fee could be one point equal to 1%.

P

Pad: The foundations of a slab used to place a mobile home, condominium, or other construction. Also, area used for landing a helicopter.

Panel Heating: Also called a radiant heater panel. A space is built into the walls to place panel heating to heat a home, water, or a single room.

Parcel Map: A map that is less costly than a subdivision map; it is simpler and smaller (1-4 lots).

Parking Ratio: A ratio of the rentable square feet of a property divided by all the parking spaces of the property.

Participation Mortgage: A mortgage where the lender participates in the equity and/or income of the property.

Patio: A terrace or courtyard. A concrete open-air area adjoining the house.

Payoff Statement: A statement prepared by the lender that shows a description of the total amount due to retire the loan.

Penthouse: Condominium on the last or highest floor of a building.

Per Annum: Annually, per year, yearly.

Per Capita: Per person, average per person.

Per Diem: Daily, per day.

Percolation Test: A test to check for the water absorption rate of soil.

Perimeter: Lines between parcel lots.

Perpetuity: Infinite, eternal, remain forevermore.

Physical Deterioration: Known as wear and tear. Loss in value due to the property's physical wear and tear.

Piggyback Loan: A loan held jointly by two or more lenders to finance 90%. Example: A 90% loan could be split into one loan for an 80% LTV, and the second one for a 10% LTV. The smallest loan has the highest risk.

Plans: Drawing, layouts, and floor plans for a whole construction or a small part of the construction like a room.

Plywood: Material manufactured from thin layers of wood for construction.

Possession: Be in control/custody of a property.

Premium: A payment for an insurance policy. Also, a prize or bonus.

Pre-paid Interest: Interest paid in advance before the interest becomes due.

Price Fixing: The Sherman Anti-Trust Act forbids brokers from fixing the price in the area related to same-case commissions, fees, or rates.

Property Tax: An ad valorem tax on the value of a property. Based on the millage rate.

Purchase Money Mortgage (PMM): When the seller becomes the lender. A loan made by a seller to a buyer. The seller is the mortgagor, and the buyer is the mortgagee.

Q

Quadrant: Instrument that measure altitudes. A quadrant measures 90 degrees, or one fourth of a circle. Two roads intersecting create a quadrant.

Quarter Section: Contains 40 acres. One fourth of a section (one section has 160 acres/4=40 acres).

Quasi: Something that looks alike; it's similar but not the same.

Quit Asset: Same as a liquid asset. Example: Cash, cash equivalent or anything that can be changed into cash quickly, such as account receivables, marketable securities, etc.

R

Real Estate: Estate involving land and/or a house or building.

Regression: A return, decline, or fall. A reduction in value of an appraisal when other properties in the comparable report are lower and affect the value of the subject property.

Rent: A periodic payment for the right of use and occupation of the property or land. The tenant pays the landlord.

Right of Survivorship: See joint tenancy.

Rail: A horizontal bar, a protective barrier.

Ramp: Commonly used for people with wheelchairs. A slope or inclined plane used to enter and exit many businesses and homes.

Ranch: Large area of land with a house. A farm for raising animals.

Rate Index: A rate serving as a benchmark index to calculate the interest rate that banks charge on loans.

Rate of Return: The annual rate of return of an investment. Example: Dividends, stocks, investment properties, etc.

Real Estate Board: Private professional organization. Group of real estate agents and brokers with the intention of helping each other in a specific area. Example: National Association of Realtors.

Real Estate Broker: Same as broker. Principal broker of a real estate office.

Reassessment: Review, reconsideration of the value of the property for tax purposes.

Receipt: A delivery of notice that proves someone will deliver something. Example: When a realtor gives condo documents to a buyer, the agent must give them a dated receipt because the buyer has three business days to cancel in the cancelation period.

Rescission of a Contract: An unmaking or unwinding of a contract between the buyer and seller.

Reconditioning: When a property is renovating for the better.

Recorded Map: A map stored in the public record of the county.

Recording Fee: A fee that the county court office charges to record any deed, mortgage, note, title, etc.

Release Clause: A clause that frees a buyer from a debt. If the buyer pays all their debt, they will be released from the lien or mortgage.

Renewal: Commonly used on leases. Example: A tenant and landlord decide to renew the lease for another year. A broker and landlord decide to renew the rental listing agreement and the broker receives a commission.

Right of Anticipation: The right to pay in advance before the due date without any penalty.

Right of First Refusal (ROFR): Contractual right that gives the holder the option to enter in the transaction with an individual or entity before anyone else can. Like a call option.

Rollover Loan: A renewable loan. An automatically renewable loan when the loan is not paid in full.

Running with the Land: A written promise for the use of the land. Agreement that runs with the land.

S

Safety Clause: A clause that protects the broker or listing agent after the listing contract expires. If the buyer and seller decide to wait until the contract expires to complete the purchase contract, the safety clause saves the agent/broker's commission.

Sales Associates: A licensed real estate agent who represents a buyer and/or a seller in a real estate transaction. Sales associates cannot work on their own; they are licensed to work under a broker.

Sales Presentation: A presentation must be pleasant, direct, and effective for buyers, sellers, or investors. An important tool every agent should have on paper and electronically.

Salvage Value: The value of a property at the end of its useful life expectancy.

Satisfaction: A loan that is paid in full; the fulfillment of a loan or debt. Also, clients' satisfaction.

Sea Level: Measure of elevation compared to the sea's surface.

Search: Refers to search properties for a buyer such as title search, lien search, etc.

Secondary Finance: A second mortgage, a subordination loan, or a second loan.

Share Appreciation Mortgage: When the lender or bank, in exchange for a lower interest rate, participates in the profit of a property when and if the property is sold.

Shingles: A type of roof covering that consists of overlapping flat elements in a rectangular shape.

Situs: A preferred place, a location.

Small Business Administration (SBA): A United States governmental agency that provides support to entrepreneurs and small businesses. Gives assistance in the event of disaster to help entrepreneurs and companies. Example: With the Covid-19 pandemic, the SBA provided economic recovery loans and grants. The SBA has multiple other programs for entrepreneurs and companies.

Special Assessment: An extra fee on top of the association fee used in many condominium associations for special improvements to the building. Example: A new roof, flooring, etc.

Short Term Capital Gain: A profit made in a short-term investment that is held for less than one year. Example: Sales from stocks, properties, bonds, etc.

Short Term Lease: Usually on residential properties. Example: Any lease for a term less than 6 months, such as month to month. Used for companies like Airbnb.

Speculator: Person who invests in property, stocks, and other ventures with the expectation of making a profit.

Spouse: Husband or wife, partner.

Statute of Fraud: Requires that certain contracts be in writing and signed by all parties involved in the agreement to be sufficient as evidence of the contract.

Structure: Construction, building, house.

Subcontractor: Person or entity that signs an agreement to perform work.

Syndicate: A group of people that forms an organization with the expectation of making a profit and/or to foster a mutual benefit.

T

Tangible Value: Something that can be touched that is real and measurable. Example: Property, land, inventory, etc.

Tax District: Local government tax entity that charges for regular property tax situated in a projected or accepted revenue development zone.

Taxes: Contribution to the state, federal government, county, or city that a person or entity pays for business profits, services, transactions, etc.

Tax Exemption: Status that holds certain entities exempt from taxation, either partially or in full. Example: Non-profit, religious, veterans, and senior organizations.

Tax Search: Research on the status of a property to establish that is clear of past tax liabilities.

Tax Stamps: When a property is sold, it must pay this tax to transfer the property. It is $0.70 cents for each $100. Example: 100,000/100=1000*.70=$700 or the sales price multiplied by $.007.

Tenant at Sufferance: When the lease between the tenant and landlord expires and the tenant continues living on the property; renews the lease prior to the landlord requesting the tenant leave.

Tenant in Severalty: Only one property owner; unshared ownership.

Terms: In a real estate contract, how the contract will proceed; finance terms, down payment, deposits, etc.

Thermal: Relating to heat. Example: Thermal water, thermal conductivity, capacity.

Third Party: A party who is not in the contract. Example: Many real estate contracts require a third-party approval when the buyer is not buying with cash.

Tile: A ceramic material used for floors and many other areas of a property like bathrooms, kitchens, walls, floors, etc.

Title Company: A company that does the closing of properties and businesses for buyers and sellers. Title companies do many searches like title, lien, and municipal searches to ensure the title is in good standing to close.

Ton: A unit of measure equal to 2000 pounds or 910 kg.

Town: An area normally smaller than a city; an urban area.

Townhouse: Townhome, row houses, usually made of two or three floors.

Township Strips: When the horizontal and the vertical lines intersect, forming a square.

Tract: A large area, region, or zone.

Trade Area: An area designed for commercial business purposes to attract customers. The market area.

Trailer Park: A community intended for trailer homes with many facilities like water, sewer, and electricity.

Triple Net: Known as triple net lease (NNN), triple-N. The tenant pays the basic rent plus other costs like insurance, property taxes, and more.

Two Hour Door: A door that is resistant to fire for at least two hours.

Two Hour Wall: Wallboard panel that is resistant to fire for at least two hours. Panel is on each side of the steel stud rather than wood.

U

Unavoidable Clause: When circumstances occur that are without fault or negligence such as death or illness.

Undisclosed Principal: When the person used an agent to negotiate and did not disclose their identity.

Undivided Interest: All owners have an equal right to enjoy the whole property, co-ownership.

Unearned Increment: An increase in the value of land, a building, or a property without having done any improvements to the property.

Unencumbered: Free and clear title of a property.

Unimproved Land: Virgin land with no improvements or buildings.

Unincorporated Area: A city that is independent from the county. Area that does not belong to the county. Example: The city of Coral Gables is in Miami Dade county, but has its own city government, police, firefighters, etc.

Unsecured: A loan with no collateral.

V

Vacancy: Available units for rent, not occupied.

Vacancy Factors: An indicator of the rate or percentage of the number of units available.

Vacate: Leave, move, get out of the property.

Valid: Legal efficacy. Example: A valid contract, a valid theory, a valid argument.

Valuation: An estimate of what something would sell for, like a house or a business by a person who knows such as an appraiser.

Variable Interest Rate: An interest rate that moves up and down depending on the index market.

Variable Expense: An expense that is not fixed every month such as property management fees that are based on the occupancy of the building.

Vent: An outlet that permits air, liquid, or gas to pass through a small space.

Venture Capital: Usually a capital investment on a new or expanded business, a project that has significant risk.

Villa: A country estate. Could be rural or suburban. Usually single-level homes with homeowner associations such as a townhouse. The villa has shared common areas.

Voluntary Alienation: The voluntary transfer of residency rights or the deed of a property between the buyer and the seller; could be a sale, gift, or dedication.

W

Wages: Payment, remuneration, or salary for a job on an hourly, daily, weekly, or biweekly amount.

Waive: Surrender, renounce, abandon a benefit or claim. Not to demand.

Wall Tile: Wall built of tile, usually in a bathroom and some kitchens to create a decorative design.

Warehouse: Used for storage or for commercial warehouse offices, industrial areas, or to rent for a short period of time.

Well: A tunnel drilled into the ground to find water, oil, or natural gas.

Wild Instrument: Any instrument found in the chain of title. Example: The mortgagor has no record of the property.

Witness: A witness is needed for all real estate closings. Some documents such as the note, deed, and more need to be attested to record the sale. A witness must be an adult and mentally competent.

Wood Frame Construction: The predominant construction material for properties in the U.S. is wood construction.

Writ of Ejectment: An action against a tenant who fails to pay rent; landlord files a claim to get possession of the property.

X

X: Roman numeral for ten. A check mark used on many contracts.

X-Bracing: X-bracing has been used in construction for more than a hundred years. Could be made of metal or wood. Many engineers use X-bracing for construction.

Y

Yacht Basin: Place where boats may be anchored.

Yard Lumber: Lumber used for construction and building purposes.

Z

Zero Side Yard: A construction that is built on the side boundary line to get the most benefit from the square footage.

Zoning: Municipal and local laws that regulate, govern, and determine what should be built in the area.

Zoning Variance: A variance or change from the rules established in the municipality for how land can be used. It is a concession to a zoning restriction to permit use of the land beyond the requirements.

Chapter 8

Success Action Planner

Bonus gifts for you!

- 2 Action to do lists

- 5 Notes

- 1 Tenant Application

- 1 Open House sign in form

- 1 Checklist for buyers/tenants

- 1 Checklist for sellers/landlords

- 1 Form for buyers/tenants to choose the property

- Questionnaire

List of Tasks/To Do Lists

Action To Do List	When	Priority

List of Tasks/To Do Lists

Action To Do List	When	Priority

Notes:

Notes:

_____

_____

_____

_____

_____

_____

_____

_____

_____

_____

_____

_____

_____

_____

_____

_____

_____

_____

_____

_____

Notes:

_____

_____

_____

_____

_____

_____

_____

_____

_____

_____

_____

_____

_____

_____

_____

_____

_____

_____

_____

Notes:

_____

_____

_____

_____

_____

_____

_____

_____

_____

_____

_____

_____

_____

_____

_____

_____

_____

_____

_____

_____

Notes:

_____

_____

_____

_____

_____

_____

_____

_____

_____

_____

_____

_____

_____

_____

_____

_____

_____

_____

_____

Tenant Application

Tenant Name 1: _____ Telephone _____

Date of Birth: _____ DL# _____ SS# _____

Tenant Name 2: _____ Telephone _____

Date of Birth: _____ DL# _____ SS# _____

Residential History for the Last 2 Years

Address Present Tenant 1: _____

Date you moved in: _____ Date you left: _____

Owner Name: _____ Tel: _____ Rent $ _____

Reason for move: _____

Previous Address: _____

Time of Residence: _____

Have you and/or Co-applicant ever been evicted? Yes _____ NO _____
If the answer is yes, explain _____

Have you had a bankruptcy? _____ Date? _____

Address Present Tenant 2: _____

Date you moved in: _____ Date you left: _____

Owner Name: _____ Tel: _____ Rent $ _____

Reason for move: _____

Previous Address: _____

Time of Residence: _____

Have you and/or Co-applicant ever been evicted? Yes _____ NO _____
If the answer is yes, explain _____

Have you had a bankruptcy? _____ Date? _____

Automobile Information

Tag: _____ Plate# _____ Model _____

Tag: _____ Plate# _____ Model _____

In Case of an Emergency

Name: _____ Relation: _____ Phone: _____

Address: _____

Name: _____ Relation: _____ Phone: _____

Address: _____

Name: _____ Relation: _____ Phone: _____

Address: _____

Employment History

Company Applicant 1: _____ Supervisor: _____

Address: _____ Phone: _____

Start Date: _____ Position: _____ Gross weekly salary $ _____

Company Applicant 2: _____ Supervisor: _____

Address: _____ Phone: _____

Start Date: _____ Position: _____ Gross weekly salary $ _____

Banking References/Optional

Bank: _____ Account# _____

Bank: _____ Account# _____

Personal References

Name: _____ Relationship: _____ Telephone: _____

Name: _____ Relationship: _____ Telephone: _____

Name: _____ Relationship: _____ Telephone: _____

Name: _____ Relationship: _____ Telephone: _____

_____,I authorize and give the right to verify by reason, the application including but not limited to credit check, criminal history, eviction civil records, owner verification, work verification; and exercise in its sole discretion to the extent so to reject this application and/or cancel any lease agreement that may be entered into between the parties pursuant to this application, whether during the term of such lease and/or any extension or renewal thereof, if the applicant has made any false statements or falsehoods in the application. Furthermore, the applicant(s) certify that it has not omitted any information from this application, in addition to any documents in the application package, exhibitions and/or annexes. I also grant the Real Estate company (add real estate company name) to investigate all information provided in this application. All relevant data found during this may be disclosed to the association and/or owner is authorized to obtain a credit report through a credit reporting agency of your choice.

Applicant's Signature: _____ Date: _____

Co-applicant's Signature: _____ Date: _____

Open House Date:____

SIGN IN FORM

BY:

No.	Name	Email	Phone
1			
2			
3			
4			
5			
6			
7			
8			
9			
10			
11			
12			
13			
14			
15			

Buyer/Tenant Checklist:

First step

- First interview ○
- Pre-qualification letter ○
- Search and auto email ○
- Showings ○
- Contract ○

Second step

1st deposit	○	Appraisal	○
2nd deposit	○	Loan commitment	○
Escrow letter	○	Approval	○
Inspections	○	Title company documents	○
Survey if needed	○	Walk-thru	○

Final Step

- Closing date ○
- Pick up my check ○
- Send a thank you postcard to my clients ○
- Ask for referals ○
- Add client on my database ○

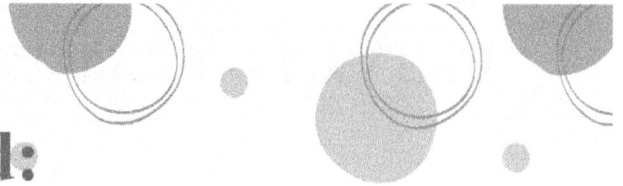

Seller/Landlord:

Checklist

Listing date: _____

Expired date: _____

Getting the Listing	Showings & Open House
☐	☐
☐	☐
☐	☐
☐	☐

Under contract	Closing
☐	☐
☐	☐
☐	☐
☐	☐

Form to Choose the Property and Get References

Form for Buyers/Tenants
Name: _____ Date: _____
Address: _____
Email:
Telephone:
Property that interested you: _____
1st property
How did you like this property? _____
2nd property
Between this property and the previous one which do you like the most?
_____
3rd and last property
Between this and the one you have liked which one do you prefer?
_____
Perfect, I see that the one you liked the most was: _____
Would you like for me to go over the numbers of this property with you?
_____
Do you prefer to go to my office, or should we do it right here?
_____
Excellent. On a scale of 1-5, what is your level of interest in this property? 1 2 3 4 5
What would change your level of interest to a 5? _____
References

Name	email	Phone

Questionnaire:

1. How do you know if a buyer is ready, willing, and able?

   _____

2. How do you know if a buyer is qualified?

   _____

3. How do you know if a tenant is qualified?

   _____

4. What phone scripts do you feel most comfortable using? Why?

   _____

   _____

5. What are the steps in a listing presentation?

   _____

6. What do you need to have or to bring to a listing presentation?

   _____

7. How do you feel when you hear NO from a seller?

   _____

8. How do you feel about rejection? How do you think you can overcome it?

   _____

   _____

9. Do you prefer to work with sellers or buyers? Why?

   _____

   _____

10. Do you prefer to work with landlords or tenants?

_____

11. Which one do you feel the most comfortable working with? Why?

_____

_____

12. Do you prefer to invest money to get clients through publicity, marketing, farming, or just investing your own time for now?

_____

13. How do you feel about delegating part of your real estate work?

_____

14. Which tasks would you delegate?

_____

15. Who could be your first assistant? Why this person?

_____

16. What qualities do they have that make you want to choose them?

_____

17. How do you feel about selling real estate virtually?

_____

18. Which clients would you work with virtually? Why?

_____

19. Which slides of the PowerPoint will you use?

_____

20. If you need other slides to adapt to your personality and company, what other slides will you add?

_____

_____

21. Which contracts do you feel the most comfortable presenting?

_____

_____

22. Describe what you learned in *The Productive Agent*:

_____

_____

_____

23. List the most common seller objections:

_____

_____

_____

24. How can I help you?

_____

_____

Send me your feedback at IvaniaAlvarado.com@gmail.com
and let me know what you think about *The Productive Agent,*
how I can improve, and how this book has helped you in your career.

Thank you and God Bless You!

Ivania

Other Books by Ivania Alvarado

The Fearless Real Estate Series

The Fearless Agent (Book 1)
The Productive Agent (Book 2)
The Successful Broker (Book 3)
Confident Contracts
Real Estate Success Action Planner

The Dreams Series

English
Your Dreams and You
Your Dreams and You Journal & Planner: 52-Week Undated Agenda and Dream Journal

Spanish
Los Sueños y Usted: Sus significados e interpretaciones
Los sueños y usted diario y planificador: Agenda de 52 semanas sin fecha y diario de sueños

Ivania Alvarado

I believe in five universal values: God, myself, family, career, and positive pleasures. I am a licensed Real Estate broker and Real Estate Instructor. I have a certificate of Business Specialist-General Business, among other studies and certificates. I graduated from Supervision and Management–Accounting Concentration from one of the biggest community colleges in the United States, Miami Dade College. I am also a student at Florida Atlantic University studying a Master of Taxation with a graduation date of December 2022. Since 1995, I have been involved in various real estate businesses including real estate sales, insurance, title companies, and a real estate school starting in 1999. The school introduced me to writing when I created the *Real Estate Manual*. This manual formed a fundamental basis for training seminars in this profession. I have had extensive experience in education and promoting salespeople by recruiting, training, advising, and educating. South Florida School of Real Estate (SFSRE.NET) has graduated more than a thousand students.

In 2001, I started writing again, contributing the "Los sueños y Usted" (Your Dreams and You) section in various magazines. That led to me writing the book *Los Sueños y Usted*. In 2004, I was inspired to create a musical CD, composed with great care and dedication, called *Los Sueños y Usted*, which became a radio and television program. In 2016, I rewrote *Los Sueños y Usted* and translated the book into English as *Your Dreams and You*. In 2021, I expanded *Your Dreams and You* into a journal and planner available in both English and Spanish, and in paperback and hardback. They are available online and in bookstores around the world. Visit IvaniaAlvarado.com for more information.

My most spiritually lucrative achievements are the help I give to religious institutions to help the homeless, Mother Teresa of Calcutta's community of the old, sick, and addicted.

Please visit the following websites for more information about my real estate journey. Thank you for your time in reading this manual and for your interest in real estate. I look forward to meeting you, working together, and leading you into the world of real estate.

www.sfsre.net

www.IvaniaAlvarado.com